SPIR

C000180187

FOOD

WONG MING~DAO

SPIRITUAL FOOD

WONG MING~DAO

20 MESSAGES
TRANSLATED BY
ARTHUR REYNOLDS

MAYFLOWER CHRISTIAN BOOKS

The Publishing Branch of
MAYFLOWER CHRISTIAN BOOKSHOPS CHARITABLE TRUST
114, Spring Road, Sholing, Southampton, Hants.

Copyright © 1983 Mayflower Christian Books

ISBN 0 907821 01 4

Cover design and line drawings by Ruth Goodridge
Printed in Finland by K. J. Gummerus Osakeyhtiö, Jyväskylä

Contents

Translator's Preface

Why was the Lord's servant, Mr Wong Ming-Dao, so greatly in demand as a preacher and teacher? Certainly the content of his preaching was not universally popular. It was a straightforward setting forth of the truths and implications of the Gospel, albeit in a style of his own. Yet not only was he held in great respect by the church with which he was associated in Peking, but also his visits would be remembered with gratitude by churches in all parts of China. I have in mind particularly, of course, the days when he was able to move around freely and to minister widely to Christians and non-Christians alike.

Two features stand out. On the one hand was the forthright and faithful nature of the message; on the other hand was the uncompromising and courageous nature of the man. He was undoubtedly a preacher with backbone. 'What did you go out into the wilderness to see? A reed shaken by the wind?'

Something of the make-up of the man can be seen in his autobiographical writings already published ('A Stone made Smooth': Mayflower Christian Books). He paints his own picture without concealing the 'warts'. Certainly not all readers would find themselves in agreement with all of Mr Wong's policies. But surely no one can doubt that here is a man of God, with the unction of the Holy Spirit, who stands out not only among the outstanding Christian leaders of China but also among the outstanding Christian leaders of the world.

The messages for the most part were given not only prior to the 23 years that he spent in prison but during the earlier years of his ministry. Their effectiveness is not hampered by considerations of time or space since they are firmly based on the authoratitive and unchangeable Word of God.

Of what do Mr Wong's messages consist? There are two strains that particularly stand out. Just as you find, in the letter of the apostle Paul to the Ephesians, that one part is made up largely of doctrine and the other part largely of conduct and behaviour, so you will perceive in the writings of Mr Wong that on the one hand he makes a powerful stand for the Faith (accompanied by warnings against false teaching) and that on the other hand he presents a strong case for maintaining a high standard of Christian living.

Most of the articles translated are taken from copies of The Spiritual Food Quarterly that I kept when my wife and I – as members of the China Inland Mission – were recalled from China in 1951. We have the author's permission to use the articles in this way.

In our view the messages of Mr Wong are singularly appropriate today and we would also like to recommend a collection of Mr Wong's later writings in English entitled 'A Call to the Church from Wang Ming-Dao.' Translated by Theodore Choy and edited by Leona F. Choy the collection is published by Christian Literature Crusade in the U.S.A.

A note of explanation should be added about our romanization of the name Wong. In the new official system of romanization, as in the old system, you still need to memorise the unusual pronunciation of certain letters or syllables. I have therefore attempted to romanize Chinese names so that readers unfamiliar with Chinese sounds may at least have a fair idea of their pronunciation in the national language. The reason why we are not here using the official spelling 'Wang' is that television advertisements are influencing people to pronounce WANG to rhyme with pang. This is not surprising, perhaps, since we also have bang and gang and hang and so on, which give it a certain consistency. So we have followed those who have adopted WONG. I have been told that one spelling is associated with 'Mandarin' and one with Cantonese. But that is not the consideration here.

Be that as it may, it is the message and not the name that matters. And in reading these messages we cannot be other than enlightened, stimulated and strengthened – nourished, in fact, with 'spiritual food', to help us in our pilgrimage. Nor do we forget that a substantial element in our paying careful attention to what our brother writes is our knowledge of the man behind the message, and of all that he and his wife have endured.

If those of us who read these messages are inspired,

as we read, to pray more diligently than in the past for our brothers and sisters in China, we shall have even more reason to offer our thanks to God that He has made possible the publication of these translations.

Arthur Reynolds.

Publishers' Preface

Two years ago we published the autobiography of Wong Ming-Dao under the title 'A Stone Made Smooth'. In the Publishers Preface we indicated that his writings would shortly be available, and we included one of his messages at the end of his book. We are delighted that the first edition of the autobiography has virtually sold out. Readers will not be disappointed with the high quality of Mr Wong's messages. They have a style that is unusual and refreshing in their penetration, insight, and simplicity. We have based the title of the book on Mr. Wong's own magazine from which the messages are taken. We have also kept his own titles for the messages, in our desire to let him speak for himself.

All quotations of scripture are from the Revised Authorised Version. *The Publishers*

1.
The distinctive colour of heaven...

Revelation 1: 12–15; 2: 17; 3: 4,5; 7: 9–14;
19: 6–8; 19: 11–14; 20: 11

The above passages of Scripture clearly point to a fact that is both important and precious. It is that the most illustrious colour in heaven is white. When the Lord Jesus appeared to John in Patmos His hair was white. To the disciples who overcame, He promised a white stone. He also promised that they should walk with Him in white garments. The twenty-four elders seated around the throne of God were wearing garments of white, while the great multitude who stood before God are described as those who 'have washed their robes and made them white in the blood of the Lamb'. At the marriage of the Lamb, on a day

1

The most illustrious colour in heaven is white

yet to come, the bride of the Lamb (i.e. the Church) will also be wearing linen clothes that are clean and bright. And on the day that the Lord Jesus executes judgement the horse on which He rides is a white horse. The hosts who accompany Him will also be arrayed in white. And in addition to that, the throne on which the Lord is seated to judge the world is also white. From the evidence of all these Scriptural records we can conclude without any doubt that the colour God loves is white.

What an attractive colour is white! Think of how pleasant it is to view a scene of snow! Or to gaze on garments of white! We are also well aware that where white articles are concerned it is impossible to conceal anything unclean. When you soil black or coloured clothes with mud or paint it is not easy for other people to notice the parts that have been soiled. How different it is with white garments! White is pure, attractive, honourable, beautiful, and intolerant of

2

anything unclean. This is the colour of heaven; it is the colour beloved by God.

Why does God, through His servant, set forth these things in the Scriptures? Is it not to teach us to pursue a life of purity which is worthy of our heavenly calling? If our lives are less than pure how can we stand with boldness and joy in the presence of His glory? It is because God wants us to be worthy of His calling, to be able to stand boldy in the presence of His glory, and to become the glorious Bride of the Lamb, that He teaches us while we are in the world to follow a manner of life that is like that of His Son – pure, sincere, righteous, modest, and compassionate; that is in fact perfect. This has been made plain to us in the Scriptures. 'Beloved; now we are children of God; and it has not yet been revealed what we shall be, but we know that when He is revealed, we shall be like Him, for we shall see Him as He is. And everyone who has this hope in Him purifies himself, just as He is pure' (1 John 3: 2,3).

The most important feature in the ideal life of a Christian is purity. Without purity, no matter what else you embrace in your life, you can never satisfy the heart of God. In the Church today there are those who emphasise the building of huge places of worship; there are those who emphasise doctrines; and there are those who emphasise the fulfilment of prophecy. But only rarely do you find those who emphasise purity of living. What is the result? Huge places of worship spring up; relief work is carried out; evangelistic efforts are promoted; a number of people speak in tongues; not a few acquire considerable knowledge of the Bible; various books relating to prophecy are published; and several new churches are brought into being. In spite of all that, the lives of many Christians are still full of selfishness, covetousness, deceitfulness, lying, licentiousness, envy, hatred, strife, flattery, oppression, pride, blasphemy, cursing, love of the world and pursuit of fame. The zeal and labour of the people concerned have not brought glory to the Lord; on the contrary His name has suffered reproach. In the eyes of men these people may be very zealous and very industrious. But in the eyes of God they are less than pure. They are recognised as people who belong to God, but their colour is not the distinctive colour of heaven. It is not difficult to search out zealous believers; we are reasonably successful in looking for believers with gifts and ability. But when we try to find believers who live blameless lives we discover that they are pitiably few in number. What a sad state of affairs!

The concept held by many believers is a mistaken one. They are under the impression that by showing zeal and by working hard they will be pleasing to God. But all the time they neglect the life of holiness. There are also believers who feel that by making large contributions both in money and in goods they will earn the blessing of God. It does not seem to cross their minds that a life of holiness is of far greater value than anything like that. What people in this category need to listen to is the advice that Samuel gave Saul: 'Has the Lord as great delight in burnt offerings and sacrifices, as in obeying the voice of the Lord? Behold, to obey is better than sacrifice, and to heed than the fat of rams. For rebellion is as the sin of witchcraft, and stubborness is an iniquity and idolatry.' (1 Samuel 15: 22,23).

Putting it another way, no matter how hard we work, and no matter what contributions we make, so long as we fail to obey God's commandments by neglecting to live a life of holiness, we not only fail to win God's commendation, we actually become displeasing to Him. Naturally we are not opposed to believers working diligently and we are not opposed to their zealously contributing their goods. For these are certainly the duties of Christian believers. They are the things that God requires of us. But of greater importance is the way we live. Those believers who place the emphasis on working for God and on contributing their goods must get their priorities right. They must make these things secondary to living a life of obedience and holiness.

There are churches whose discernment in matters of doctrine is extremely clear; and they have been able to correct errors which are derived from the traditions of men. But they then become self-important and they arbitrarily attack other churches; yet all the time their manner of life is in no way superior to that of others. At times it is worse.

Individual believers fall into the same error as churches corporately. Because they have certain gifts not possessed by others, or because they have perceived certain aspects of truth that others have neglected, or because they have some outstanding accomplishments, they tend to despise other believers and to regard themselves as God's favourites. What they do not realise is that accomplishments alone amount to nothing in the sight of God.

But suppose we do live a life of holiness, does it mean that we can boast of it? Indeed not. We are merely doing our duty. It has neither virtue nor merit. If we live a life of holiness it means that we are grateful to God for His grace. To boast of superiority is simply giving evidence that our holiness is deficient. We are guilty of pride. Becoming holier means also becoming humbler.

Although it is but rarely that we come across believers who are at all like the Lord Jesus, our Lord Jesus did not because of this lower His standards. God's requirement is still holiness. For the distinctive colour of heaven is still white. If we do not wear white garments and walk with Him in white we shall neither reign with Him nor sit with Him to execute judgement. ' . . . beseech you to walk worthy of the calling with which you were called' (Ephesians 4: 1). 'As He who has called you is holy, you also be holy in all your conduct' (1 Peter 2: 15).

2.
Be slow to speak...

James 1:19

'Therefore, my beloved brethren, let every man be swift to hear, slow to speak, slow to wrath'.

'Be slow to speak!' There are many things of which you see only one side; the other side remains hidden. There are many matters of which you know only a small part; of the large part that remains you are ignorant. If you rashly make a categorical statement based on the small part that you see or the small part that you know, you will hardly avoid being laughed at or looked down on. In fact, if the day comes eventually when you can see both sides, or when you become acquainted with the whole of the matter, you will greatly regret the words which today you give utterance! Be slow to speak!

Sometimes you may observe that a certain person has a certain bad quality and you then regard his or her as being totally bad. But it may well be that he or she has many good qualities that you have never observed. On the other hand you may observe that a certain person has a good quality and you then regard him as being totally good. But it may well be that he has many bad qualities that you have never observed. If you form a judgement that a particular person is bad – or good – by observing only one of his actions will you not yourself be exercising an evil influence? Be slow to speak!

You may sometimes hear someone commend a certain person as good, whereas he is not good like that at all. It is simply that those who flatter him fabricate untruths or exaggerate their words to eulogise him. If you are not careful you will blindly follow others in praising him, and you yourself will make a great mistake. Be slow to speak!

You may sometimes hear someone criticize a certain person as bad, whereas he is not bad like that at all. It is simply that those who dislike him want to spoil his good name. If you are not careful you will blindly follow others in describing him as bad, and you will thus become guilty of slander and you will be causing others to suffer harm. Be slow to speak!

Not a little of what you hear is purely rumour. Though much of it may have been based on fact, after it has been passed on through the mouths of several people, what is reported differs appreciably from the original happening. If you hear a rumour and then, without investigating whether it is true or false you pass it on simply as you heard it, you may easily become one who is guilty of spreading false rumours. Be slow to speak!

Not a little of what you hear is purely rumour

Sometimes you may see people fail in certain ways. Without considering the difficulties with which they had to contend you assert boldly that if you had been in their position you would not have failed as they did. Perhaps one day you have to contend with the very same difficulties and you also fail in the same way. Will you not blush with shame? Be slow to speak!

People sometimes ask you to do something for them, and without seriously thinking it over to see whether you can do it or not you promise effusively to do it for them. But when the time comes you fail to carry out your promise. As a consequence those concerned are inconvenienced and disappointed while you yourself lose people's confidence. You have to eat your own words. You harm others and you harm yourself. What a grave miscalculation. Be slow to speak!

It sometimes happens that you meet someone and have a long conversation with him. You get the impression that he is sincere and reliable, and that he loves both the Lord and other people. You regard him as a good friend and you share with him confidential matters. But after a while you discover that he is self-seeking and dangerous and that he had only enquired about your private affairs in order to make use of you. What a grievous loss you will suffer! Your regret will be indescribable! Be slow to speak!

Sometimes one of your friends will quite unintentionally make some remark that offends you. Or he may do something that offends you. From the beginning he never had the slightest intention of hurting you, but you misunderstood him and thought that he had caused you trouble purposely, so you say many things about him that cause him acute embarrassment. Later on you discover that he had indeed spoken without the slightest evil intent. What remorse you will suffer that you have offended your friend! Be slow to speak!

Sometimes you are listening to someone talking and when he has uttered only a few sentences you are convinced that what he says is wrong and you immediately contradict him. If only you waited until he finished you might fully agree with him. I have frequently seen foolish people like this. Be slow to speak!

Sometimes you want urgently to get something done and you exert yourself to do it. If it is not essential to speak about it before you do it, then don't be in a hurry to do so. If you are successful that is excellent. But if by chance you fail you will at least avoid ridicule. Be slow to speak!

When people are happy and excited it is easy to talk at random so that the words pour out of their mouth like a river. But this can easily be followed by tears. Be slow to speak!

Never forget that the words that proceed from your mouth have a strong bearing on your own character, they have a strong bearing on the welfare of others, and they have a strong bearing on the glory of God.

The Devil wants to use your words to lead you astray. Evil men will use your words to bring you harm. Mature people will use your words to determine what kind of person you are. And those around you will be influenced by your words to receive either benefit or harm. Be slow to speak!

The causes of our weaknesses and the causes of our failures are all known to God. That is why, in the Bible, He teaches us the way we should take. 'Therefore, my beloved brethren, let every man be swift to hear, slow to speak, slow to wrath' (James 1: 19).

3.
Small things and big things...

Luke 16:10

There is a concept, prevalent among Christians today, that is totally misleading. It is to the effect that it is only the big and important things in life that should be done well; in insignificant matters it is of little moment whether they are done well or not. Alongside this is the view that so long as you are not guilty of grievous sins, you may relax your standards in minor affirs without doing a great deal of harm. A viewpoint as erroneous as this can certainly spread widespread damage.

Big things are normally made by putting together many small things. Imposing buildings are made up of countless pieces of wood and stone and brick. In any

Imposing buildings are made up of countless small pieces

major project there are innumerable small component parts. If a man cannot do well in handling small things how can he hope to achieve anything big? It is necessarily in small matters that a man must learn to be faithful and diligent and painstaking; to be careful about detail; to endure and persevere; and not to make a start unless he can see the way to finish.

Having learned his lessons in small things he will be equipped to face big things. The words spoken by our Lord are words of authority: 'He that is faithful in that which is least is faithful in much' (Luke 16:10).

The same argument can be applied to wrongdoing. When a person makes a habit of speaking untruths and of being deceitful in small things how can you expect him to be sincere and upright in big things? When a person is habitually avaricious and careless in small things, how can you expect him to be incorruptible and honourable in big things? When a person takes advantage of others in small things he will certainly seek private advantage in big things.

Those who are self-seeking, covetous, fierce and dissolute in small things will certainly be incapable of sincerity, compassion, honesty, meekness, purity and soberness in greater matters. Look at a man's behaviour in small matters and you are well-placed to judge his character. The Lord Jesus long ago made this clear: 'He that is unjust in the least is unjust also in much' (Luke 16:10).

When a devout believer with a good character stumbles, and falls from his high position, you will find that it generally began with something small. If a person commits a small sin, and does not soon repent and confess it, he will soon be committing that sin as a habit. The devil does not bother himself about the possibility of believers committing great sins; he only fears their committing small sins. So when devout saints give expression to just a little doubt or covetousness or lust or envy or hatred or pride or deceit, they must quickly repent of it. Otherwise the sins in their lives will increase and they will be less and less desirous of worshipping God. In the end they will turn their back on God and commit sins that at one time they never dreamed of.

Saul, the first King of Israel, is a notable example. When God first chose him to be king he had some outstanding virtues. If we read the passage 1 Samuel 9–11 carefully we can see that he was then humble, obedient, industrious and persevering; he sympathized with his parents; he was large-hearted and he returned good for evil. He was truly a virtuous king. During the years that followed, however, he indulged in various sins and did not quickly repent of them. On the contrary he disguised them. From that time on his fall was inevitable. In the end he became envious of those who were worthy and skilful; he returned evil for good and he was guilty of killing the priests. He eventually asked a woman who communicated with evil spirits to call up the spirit of a dead man – a procedure that in the eyes of God was akin to rebellion. As a result he lost his life in the battlefield, his body was taken by the Philistines, and his end was disaster and shame.

In summer time it is common for streams to pour down from the mountains and for the level of the rivers to rises. However, with dykes on both banks the water does not overflow to spread disaster. Yet the volume is small and it does not seem greatly to matter. However, after the water has been pouring out for an hour or two the opening grows larger, and it becomes beyond human strength to block it. Within a matter of hours the water overflows in ever increasing quantity and inundates thousands of acres of good land. Yet the original cause of this great calamity was nothing more than a small hole in the dyke. Does it now show us that small aberrations are potentially devasting?

When a strong healthy man is at work he may inadvertently scratch his hand. If he does not immediately apply an antiseptic it may become poisoned and may even require amputation. It can even endanger life. Who dares to say that small things are unimportant?

We are frequently confronted by disasters resulting from fires. Within half a day a large building may become a ruin, and valuable property may be turned to ashes. The people involved may lose all that they possess and their lives may be blighted. But when calamitous fires like this are traced to their source it is found, not infrequently, that it is due to a lighted cigarette being thrown away unthinkingly on a pile of waste paper. The fire quickly spreads.

Let us turn to greater issues. When war breaks out between two States it is often as a result of a trivial musunderstanding or a minor clash. The outcome, however, is a major calamity, with whole States and peoples being drawn into the whirlpool. Unnumbered heroes die on the battlefield. The lives of potentially useful citizens are wasted. Women become widows and children become orphans. Property is turned into ashes and houses become ruins. If only, at the beginning, one side had been willing to acknowledge being in the wrong, and given way, these tragic consequences would not have followed.

No matter who is involved – individuals, or families, or society, or a nation – all calamities such as wars develop from small beginnings. Even trivial sins, then, are to be feared. Only the wise can discern the potential consequences of seemingly insignificant events. Yet most people do not take these things to heart; they regard them as unimportant. Only when a major calamity occurs do they stir themselves to try and retrieve the situation. But by then it is already too late.

Once we understand this truth we ought to be

always on the alert, as if treading on thin ice, lest we become guilty of seemingly trivial wrongdoing. Whenever we fall into sin we should take immediate action, just as when a hole appears in a dyke or when a fire breaks out.

Do not retain the slightest evil thought! Do not utter a single ungodly word! Do not participate in even one wicked act. Do not pay even one visit to places that ought to be avoided. Never wear the mask of pretence. Never give way to violence. Never influence others for evil. Do not cause other people on your account to suffer loss. The fact is, we ought to fear little sins as much as big sins. We ought to beware of little dangers as much as big dangers. For only those who avoid falling into little sins can avoid falling into big sins. Only those who take precautions against little dangers can safely avoid big dangers.

Then what about our duties? We ought never to neglect the lesser duties, the minor tasks, and the insignificent deeds of kindness. Even the smallest tasks must be carried out diligently and faithfully, no less than the more important tasks. Whenever you have an opportunity to do something small on behalf of others, or to give a little help to others, or to impart some comfort to others, grasp that opportunity firmly and do not let it go.

Our *major* acts of benevolence are of course observed by our fellow-men, but it is the Lord who observes our minor acts of benevolence. Our flesh invariably pines to do big things and to be seen by the world and to perform acts of kindness acclaimed by the crowd, but what our Lord pays attention to is whether we are faithful in small things. so long as we are faithful in small things, irrespective of whether we have opportunity to do big things or not, we shall be commended by the Lord. But if we are not faithful in small things, no matter what impressive accomplishments we can present to the world, we shall be reproved rather than commended by the Lord. His words are clear: 'He that is faithful in that which is least is faithful also in much: and he that is unjust in the least in unjust also in much'.

Among those who will receive rewards, in the Kingdom of God, there will undoubtedly be many of whom today we take little account. They may possess no particular skill or ability, and they may fail to attract the attention of the world, but they make full use of all the gifts that they do possess, and in the eyes of the Lord they are faithful. He will surely say to them, 'Well done, thou good and faithful sevant!'

At the same time there are undoubtedly many in the church who are highly respected, and who are regarded by ordinary believers as 'pillars' in the church, who will fail to merit award. They will in fact merit rebuke, for the work they do does not spring from sincerity and love, but from a desire to be prominent. What the world looks for is 'bigness' but what the Lord looks for is 'genuineness'.

It is not that we are opposed to people doing great things for the Lord. He once said to His disciples, 'He that believeth in me, the works that I do shall he do also; and greater works than these shall he do, because I go unto my Father' (John 14:12). So long as we are faithful in small things the Lord in due time will give us big things to do, and without doubt we shall be able to carry them out satisfactorily. But if you set your mind only on big things, and do not faithfully carry out the small things, I can only be concerned about you.

If it is our aim to be acceptable to the Lord then we ought faithfully to carry out the duties that lie before us irrespective of whether we are commended by men or not, or even whether anyone knows or not. Even less should we stop to analyse whether the work we do is big or small – high or low. If you have a duty to perform, then do it. Be willing to take responsibility and be ready to exert yourself. For the sake of the Lord go and do those things that others are unwilling to do. It is the Lord who will honour and praise you.

Those whom the Lord wants to use greatly He will constantly put to the test. So before He entrusts the bigger responsibilities to them He first assigns to them tasks that seem small and insignificant. Some people fail to observe these tasks while others regard them as too trivial. Their eyes are still on big things. Other people are too lazy, or unprepared to humble themselves. Their eyes are still on big things.

It is the few who do not neglect the small things. They never ask whether there is any recompense. When they see work to be done they work hard and diligently to carry it out. God is testing them and he will give them bigger things to do. And one day He will exalt them to sit with Christ in the place of authority.

When the great negro Booker T. Washington was a young man he went to a certain university to apply for entrance. He was interviewed by a woman official of the university and because of immediate impressions she was unwilling to accept him. He sat there for several hours which made her very surprised. She then told him that there was a room in the unviersity which needed to be cleaned and she asked him whether he would be willing to clean it. Booker was delighted. He diligently washed the floor, he dusted the furniture, and he left the room without a speck of dust. When the official returned she used a snow-white handkerchief to wipe the furniture. Not the slightest mark of soiling was made.

She promised him a place in the university immediately and Booker regarded this as the happiest event in his life.

That woman official used this method of testing the character of Booker T. Washington. She wanted to see whether he was humble or not, whether he was diligent or not, and whether he was faithful or not in the lesser matters. Suppose he had thought to himself, 'I have no hope of being accepted for the university, why should I do this chore voluntarily?' And suppose because of such an attitude he had been unwilling to clean that room, or in doing so had done so carelessly, he would hardly have been accepted. But this young man who was faithful in small things was in time to accomplish great things. He worked for the education of negroes to the extent that he secured the respect not only of countless negroes but also of countless whites. He could hardly have imagined, as he swept that room, what a vast effect it would have on his life.

That is how God tests His children. They ask to be taught by God in the hope of doing great things for God. But God first directs them to perform a task that is menial. At this point, alas! there are those who are unwilling to humble themselves and in so doing they forfeit their usefulness in the sight of God. 'To travel far you must start nearby' said one of our philosophers, 'and to climb a high mountain you must start down below'.

'He that is faithful in that which is least', said the Lord Jesus, 'is faithful also in much.' Unless we can learn this vital lesson we have no hope whatever of achieving anything great.

4.
Repenting and believing...

Mark 1: 14,15; Acts 2: 37,38; Acts 20: 20,21

The first of the three passages concerns the call of
Jesus to the Jews at the beginning of his ministry. The
second passage is of the Gospel that Peter preached,
on the Day of Pentecost, to the Jews who had
gathered from many places. The third passage
consists of words that Paul addressed to the Ephesian
elders at Miletus. All these three New Testament
records are important, first of all, because they reveal
clearly that the doctrines proclaimed by the Lord
Jesus Christ and by Peter, the apostle to the Jews, and
that proclaimed by Paul, the apostle to the Gentiles,
are identical. They are also important because they
show that the basic doctrine they preached contained

two elements – the first was repentance and the second was believing the Gospel that Jesus died for sinners. Regarding the first of these – repentance – the words used by all three were the same. Regarding the second, although the actual expressions were different, there was no difference of meaning.

What the Lord Jesus said was, 'Believe the Gospel!' What is the Gospel? We are told by the apostle Paul. 'Moreover, brethren, I declare to you the Gospel which I preached to you . . .For I delivered to you first of all that which I also received: that Christ died for our sins according to the Scriptures, and that He was buried, and that He rose again the third day according to the Scriptures.' (1 Corinthians 15:1–4). From this we learn that believing the Gospel means believing that Jesus died a substitutionary death and that He rose from the dead. Putting it the other way round, to believe in Jesus is to believe the Gospel. The apostle Peter said, 'Repent, and let every one of you be baptised in the name of Jesus Christ . . .' On the surface it seems that Peter did nothing about believing in Jesus. But think carefully a moment! Is not being baptised in the name of Jesus an event that follows believing in Jesus as one's Saviour? Without believing in Jesus how can you be baptised in His name? Being baptised expresses our dying with Jesus, our being buried with Him, and our rising again with Him. Looking at it this way, it is necessary to have believed in the substitutionary death of Jesus and in His burial and in His resurrection. Then we come to Paul. What Paul said was: 'I kept back nothing that was helpful to you . . .testifying to Jews, and also to Greeks, repentance toward God and faith toward our Lord Jesus Christ.' It is easy to see, without further explanation, that which Paul preached was exactly the same as that which was preached by the Lord Jesus Christ and by Peter.

Without doubt those who genuinely believe in the Lord Jesus will first have repented before God. Putting it another way, it is necessary first to repent before you can speak in terms of believing in the Lord Jesus. The act of repentance does not include believing in Jesus, but believing in Jesus will certainly include repentance. How can a person who does not confess his sin, and turn from his sin, still believe in Jesus? What kind of a person would be prepared to continue living in sin and to die in sin and yet call himself the disciple of Jesus? When we preach the Gospel we must certainly preach the Gospel of Jesus having died for sinners, but we need first to make people aware of their sin and of the painful consequences of sin. We must call upon people to repent toward God. When they are aroused by the realisation of their sin, and when on account of their sin they reprove themselves and hate themselves and are ashamed of themselves and humble themselves, then we can go on and introduce them to the Saviour and to the way of salvation that God has provided for them. When they repent before God, and confess and forsake their sin, and when with the eye of faith they look away to Jesus, they will then be forgiven and saved. In the light of this we can say that all who truly believe in Jesus will have first experienced the act of repenting toward God. In other words, they are all people who have confessed and forsaken their sin. We note then that not only are repenting and believing closely related to each other but that the act of repenting is prior to the act of believing.

One of the deplorable tendencies today is for many preachers to preach the doctrine erroneously. All that they preach is the doctrine of believing in the Lord and being saved, but they do not preach the doctrine of repentance. They have not awakened people to a sense of their sin, let alone led them to confess it and forsake it. Although these preachers preach about Jesus having died for sinners, their listeners have not yet become conscious of their own sin – and even less have they confessed their sin before God and repented of it – so naturally they are not in a position to put their trust in Jesus. So if you are concerned with people of this kind who indicate that they wish to believe in Jesus and who would like to join the church, please consider what kind of Christians they are! The best among them are those who admire what they have seen in Jesus of the 'spirit of sacrificing one's life to preserve one's integrity' . . .or who look up to the moral character of Jesus and His great personality. We neet not talk about those who have lower aims than this.

When preachers ask them whether or not they believe in Jesus, they reply 'Yes!' And they probably regard themselves as having truly believed in Jesus. But in reality all that they have known are 'the footsteps of Jesus' and that is all. Few would stop to think that believing in Jesus is one thing and that knowing 'the footsteps of Jesus' is another. All who believe in Jesus must know the footsteps of Jesus, but not all who know the footsteps of Jesus are believers in Jesus. Knowing the footsteps of Jesus is head knowledge – that is, knowing what we read about Jesus in various printed records. Believing in Jesus is truly to trust Him in one's heart, calling upon Him for salvation. For salvation is the result of our truly trusting Him. Alas! Many people confuse the two concepts and they regard knowledge of the footsteps of Jesus as being identical with having faith in Jesus.

Even more lamentable is that many preachers

themselves regard the people who know the footsteps of Jesus as being believers in Jesus. I can cite a widespread practice as evidence of this. It is that when many churches are examining those who have asked them for baptism, the questions they ask mostly have to do with knowledge of what is in the Bible. So long as the applicants can answer these questions they are accepted for baptism. Once accepted for baptism they are acknowledged to be believers in Jesus. As to whether they have repented before God or not, and as to whether they have truly trusted in Jesus or not, there are few who bother to ask such questions. So the practice has developed of only enquiring about Bible knowledge, while failing to ask whether the person concerned has truly repented before God. On the strength of that, the applicant has been received into the church. This procedure has occurred so often as to cause me great grief.

What are the results of using dubious methods of work? Many names are added to the church register; the regular collections are enlarged; the preachers are eulogised as 'fishers of men' and as 'great evangelists'; and there is an increase in the number of tares that grow amongst the wheat. Many are added to the church who are bogus and yet appear to be genuine, who do not believe yet give the appearance of believing. God's name is blasphemed by the world, and the church becomes a 'nest of the Devil'. Although it is not for one reason alone that the church becomes currupt, one of the major reasons is certainly the practice of receiving into the church those who have neither repented nor put their trust in the Lord. Unless those who work for the Lord show a change of heart in this matter the future of the church will not be bright.

I add a warning. I urgently call on those who regard

themselves as Christians to look at themselves carefully and to ask themselves before God whether they have sincerely repented and believed. If your life is dominated by sin; if your thoughts, words, and deeds are still full of unbelief, unrighteousness, deceit, lying, covetousness, envy, hatred, pride, selfishness and violence, and so on, and if you are still not ashamed of these things, then I tell you, you have certainly not yet repented and believed in the Lord. Not only so, but since you constantly hear the truth and you know that these sins are what God hates, yet you still call yourself a believer, then your sins are even greater than those of others differently placed. You will certainly receive the greater punishment. Yet if today you awaken to a sense of your own sin and repent before God, if you acknowledge and forsake your sin, if you seek God's compassion and salvation and put your trust in the Lord Jesus, it will not be too late. But if you harden your heart, having the name of a Christian but not being a Christian in reality, then sooner or later you will bitterly regret having deceived yourself and having brought about you own destruction. It grieves me to see such a possibility, so I cry unto you earnestly, warning you of your danger and hoping against hope that you will awaken. Are you prepared to receive my warning?

5.
A great prophet and a self-abasing commander...

2 Kings 5: 8–17

Naaman was a man with authority, power, position and wealth. He was an illustrious and awe-inspiring commander in the kingdom of Aram. Had he not contracted leprosy, and urgently sought healing, it would have been quite unthinkable for him to go out of his way to call on a servant of God. By coming to God's servant he had an excellent opportunity to get to know God and to be blessed by Him. But before he could experience such a blessing he had to humble himself. For this he needed a teacher. The responsibility for this fell naturally on the shoulders of Elisha, the servant of God. Word came to Elisha that Naaman had brought horses and chariots and changes of raiment, and that he had gone with a letter to the king of Israel. Elisha also heard that the king of Israel was vexed to the extent of tearing his clothes. Elisha wanted, on the one hand, to serve the king of Israel and, on the other hand, to heal Naaman. So he sent a messenger to the king, saying, 'Why have you torn your clothes, let him come to me now, and he shall know that there is a prophet in Israel.' Naaman was not only a powerful and awe-inspriing leader, with authority and power and position and wealth, he was also the honoured guest of a sovereign state. If anyone in Israel wished to have an audience with him he would have to show great respect and reverence, hoping in that way to gain his favour.

But contrary to all expectation Elisha did not go and pay his respects to Naaman; what he did was to make Naaman come and see him. To the king of Israel he said, 'Let him come now to me!' He did not refer to Naaman as 'Commander', he referred to him simply as 'the man'. Was this an indication of arrogance on the part of Elisha? Certainly not! Although in the eyes of men Naaman was a powerful leader, in the eyes of God he was simply one man among many men, and no more. Elisha was the servant of God, so when he looked at Naaman he did so with the eyes of God and not with the eyes of men. That is why he referred to Naaman simply as 'the man'. God is willing to bestow His blessing on all who seek Him, and Naaman was no exception. But first of all God wanted to teach him the lesson of humility.

Naaman passed the first test without difficulty. In other words he was perfectly willing to take his horses and his chariots and to stand outside the door of Elisha's house. The fact that Naaman could learn the first lesson so quickly was of course because he had contracted leprosy and urgently sought healing. So as soon as the prophet called him he came. After he had learnt this first lesson God had to lead him a step further. He had to learn a second lesson. 'Elisha sent a messenger to him, saying, Go and wash in Jordan seven times, and your flesh will be restored to you, and you shall be clean' (5: 10).

Consider the situation. Here was a commander held in great honour who had not hesitated to come and call on Elisha – a procedure that was already extremely difficult. It never occurred to him that on his arrival at the house of Elisha he would be treated so coldly. Previously, no matter where he went, he was always warmly welcomed. He assumed that Elisha would receive him respectfully at the door of his house, that he would stand and call on the name of the Lord his God, wave his hand over the spot, and cure him of his leprosy. To be treated so coldy was certainly not the treatment that Naaman had expected. Yet it was exactly what Naaman needed. It was common for people with authority and power and wealth like Naaman to be proud and arrogant. He urgently needed someone to teach him humility, for only by humbling himself could he experience the grace of God. 'For God resists the proud but gives grace unto the humble'. So Elisha's purpose in treating him as he did was not to humiliate him but to teach him humility, thus making it possible for him to be blessed by God.

Alas for Naaman! Although he had learnt the first lesson very well, this was not the case with the second lesson, which was much more difficult. It made him very angry that Elisha treated him so disdainfully. He made up his mind not to stay any longer and he went off in a rage. Fortunately in the end he listened to the exhortation of his servants and as a consequence he obeyed the command of the prophet to go and bathe in the river Jordan. This meant that he was cleansed of his leprosy and came to know God.

We should observe at this point that when Naaman went back to Elisha, after he had been cleansed, the prophet did not refuse to see him as he had done on the previous occasion. The reason was that Naaman had already learnt the lesson of humility and so it was no longer necessary to 'dampen his ardour'. It is to be observed also that although Naaman had previously been treated by Elisha rather coldly, this no longer bothered him and he was full of gratitude to the prophet. Clearly he had become very humble. 'Now I know,' he said, 'that there is no God in all the earth but in Israel' (5: 15). These words show us that Naaman's eyes had now been opened. He saw what he had not seen previously. And now he had not only come to know God but he also wanted to give glory to God. This was of far greater value and of far greater importance than simply being cleansed of leprosy. Yet both of these blessings had come to him because he had humbled himself before God.

There are prominent people in the world today who have authority and power and wealth and reputation like Naaman. In the eyes of the world they are great and honourable, but in the eyes of God they are as needy as Naaman. They suffer from the leprosy of sin. And they do not know God. Among these people are some who are already conscious of their need and they are already seeking God's grace. There are others who are in trouble and who seek deliverance and comfort from God. Then there are others who have been influenced by Christian believers and want to hear the Gospel. In a situation like that they can be blessed just like Naaman was. But there must be preachers within reach like Elisha who can convince such people of their sin and of their need, and who can go on to tell them of the salvation of the Lord Jesus Christ, so that they repent and believe.

Alas! Many preachers today have their sights set on gain and fame, and their outlook is extremely small (lit. their circle of vision is no larger than a bean). Unlike Elisha they are incapable of teaching anyone situated like Naaman by 'damping his ardour'. On the contrary they vie with one another to be first in attracting his attention and in seeking to help him.

It is true that people with authority and power and wealth are found amongst those who repent and believe. But spiritually they are babes. They need to be guided and nurtured by the servants of God. So if there are faithful servants of God at hand to guide them, they may make steady progress and become meat for the Master's use.

But there are some preachers who are far from teaching them the truth; they strive to draw such people into their own church and in order to exploit their position and their wealth. They flatter them; they invite them to preach; they elect them as deacons and elders. The fact is, these people are but babes in Christ. On the one hand they have not yet come to an understanding of the truth; on the other hand they are unfamiliar with the ways of Satan. It may be that they are amenable to flattery; they are naturally elated to be offered privileges. They begin to think of themselves as pillars in the church and as great men in the kingdom of heaven. They are no longer capable of recognising their own needs and shortcomings. On the contrary they think of themselves as having grown mature and they believe that God can now use them. Yet they are still impoverished and immature Christians. It is impossible for them to make spiritual progress and they are no longer open to receive God's

For the Christian life may be compared to rowing upstream

blessing. Unable to go forward they can only go backwards. For the Christian life may be compared to rowing up stream.

The preachers for their part are highly elated. Have they not secured the services of people with prestige and influence and wealth? Preachers who can draw on the resources of prominent men like this are open to receive benefits from all directions. But the prominent people can only suffer harm.

Ordinary people who have neither prestige nor wealth nor standing also repent and believe in the Lord. And I have noticed this. In most cases, after they have become Christians, they make spiritual progress. Sometimes it is so remarkable that everybody can see it. On the other hand when those who have standing and influence believe in the Lord it often happens that they fail to make spiritual progress. This is because they have been hindered by preachers who flatter them and who seek to ingratiate themselves with them. In this way the Christian life of many has been seriously hindered. It makes one weep even to think of it.

Is it surprising that preachers like this are found in the church today? Not in the least. We have to ask the question, how many preachers today have been truly chosen by God? How many of them can overcome the temptation to seek the material benefits of gain and fame? Is it not a fact that there are even preachers who have not yet repented and who are not yet saved? Preaching is just a means of livelihood.

There are certainly many good preachers who are seeking to glorify God; they are seeking the lost and they are building up the church. But in one respect they greatly err. They take the view that in order to further the work of God they must get the help of people of influence and reputation and wealth. They bend every effort to get hold of such people and to draw them into the church. In such a situation they are reluctant to correct the faults of these people and they fail to teach them basic doctrine. Obviously these preachers are not in the same category as those who curry favour with prominent people in their own interests. Nevertheless they can still do considerable harm.

I urge all those who work for God to look well at the example of Elisha, neither coveting riches nor currying favour with those who have power. No matter what the standing of those who come to you to hear the Gospel, or to seek spiritual help, on no account permit yourself the hope of gaining something from them. Concentrate your thoughts on treating them with compassion and on giving them the guidance they need. Only in this way can you be a faithful servant of God and glorify Him.

Elisha refused to engage in flattery and did not hesitate to dampen Naaman's ardour, yet he was able to give guidance to Naaman and bring him to the point where he unreservedly humbled himself.

Look again at Naaman. After he had bathed in the river and been cleansed of his leprosy he went back to Elisha taking gifts, which he urged Elisha to accept. He said to Elisha, 'Now therefore, please, take a gift from your servant.' But Elisha replied, 'As the Lord lives, before whom I stand, I will receive nothing.' And although Naaman repeatedly pleaded with him, he steadfastly refused.

This episode greatly increases our respect for Elisha. Not only did he make no request for reward but even when it was offered to him he refused to accept it. Completely free of covetousness! Completely incorruptible! What great spiritual heights he reached!

There are those who recognise the greatness of Elisha in seeking no material recompense from Naaman. But they are inclined to feel that in refusing the gifts that were freely offered to him he was acting too strictly.

Once again I would warn those of you, young in the faith, who have authority and standing and wealth. Be on your guard against those preachers who flatter you and who seek to curry favour with you. Don't allow them to exploit you! Don't take it for granted that all preachers are necessarily servants of God, and that all without exception are capable of giving you spiritual help. I myself have seen young believers who have stumbled through unhelpful preachers to the point of losing their faith.

The preachers who can help you are the ones who do not flatter you. They are prepared to point out your faults and they are able to give you counsel. Such people are very rare. So when you come into contact with them you should respect them and treat them with courtesy, paying attention to their conscientious exhortations and following their advice. But how many who are trustworthy like this can be found among preachers today? Is it possible to find one in ten?

So long as you have authority and standing and wealth it will be hard for you to avoid having pressure put upon you by people who curry favour with you. You will need to watch yourself! For these flatterers will adapt themselves to your ideas, and will do all they can to please you. In a situation like this you can so easily react by becoming proud. As a new believer in the Lord it will be far easier for you to bask in adulation than to accept conscientious exhortation. But if your mind is set on escaping unhelpful influences you must learn to resist flattery and to be open to instruction that is honest and straightforward. And never be unwilling to accept words of reproof!

6.
Dangers in the present-day church...

The greatest danger to the church is not persecution. It is not attack from outside. The greatest danger to the church is corruption and deterioration within. When the church is healthy then progress and prosperity will follow naturally. Even if the church is unhappily attacked by an external force as powerful as a hurricane it will only become stronger and healthier itself.

But if the church becomes corrupt, and its inner condition degenerates, it will not be able to stand against troubles from outside, and it will inevitably collapse. Externally the church may appear to be flourishing, but like the city of Babylon it is only awaiting God's time to destroy it. The church of today is surrounded by forces of evil and has been subject to numerous attacks. But the real danger does not lie here. The real danger is found *inside* the church. Alas! Far too many believers are unaware of these dangers, which are truly formidable. And of the believers who are unaware of these inner dangers a large number are inhibited by too great a regard for other people's 'face' (ie reputation). Or it may be that the reason they are unwilling to speak out plainly is their fear of losing out in some way themselves. So although the danger in the church of this present age is very great, both the ordinary believers and their leaders are apparently unconscious of it and they are moving steadily to the inevitable end in a dream. In a frightening situation of this kind, so long as no one will stir himself to raise an outcry, the future of the church is so uncertain that no one dare forecast what will happen.

I am moved by a strong sense of mission so that I cannot do other than speak out. I will now set out for consideration some of the greatest dangers in the church of this present time.

1 Worship of Wealth

The worship of wealth is an evil phenomenon which is found all over the world. You cannot count the multitudes who see nothing and seek nothing but money. The thought of wealth has so gripped their hearts and so blinded their minds that they see neither friends not brothers nor parents nor God. Future dangers are out of their sight. In order to amass wealth they will sink to anything. They have no hesitation in harming other people; they are ready to betray friends as well as masters; they are prepared to discard their conscience; they commit sin without compunction and they will even resort to murder. The iniquities that now characterise society arise largely from the love of money. How true it is, as the Bible faithfully tells us, that 'the love of money is the root of all evil'.

The church is a body of people whom God has chosen out of a world of sin. This has important implications. It means that God's people must separate themselves from all unrighteousness and all uncleanness. They must trust in God and serve God and worship God. And they must do all this with a single mind.

But what has happened? Many of them in these days leave God, who called them, out of their reckoning. They follow the ways of the world. They begin to worship wealth. That the people of Canaan should worship idols is not in any way strange. But when the Israelites whom God mightily delivered from Egypt to do the same – that is strange indeed. Even stranger is the fact that among those who worshipped idols were the princes and the leaders of Israel. When unbelievers today worship money we are not unduly pained, for that is what we would expect. What causes us pain is that Christians worship money. And we are pained even more to find that church officers give a lead to ordinary believers in this worship of money.

People who do not believe in God, whatever their occupation, have this common propensity that they put money first. This is because they have no knowledge of the omnipotent God, and it is money, to their eyes, that represents the greatest power. So their actions are not by any means strange. Alas! So many in the church today are treading a road that is no different from the road trodden by unbelievers. Their priority is not God but wealth. Many churches, when they contemplate a particular enterprise, never think of getting down before God to pray, and to seek

His guidance and undertaking. They are only concerned with soliciting contributions in order to finance a particular project.

The strongest evidence of this 'Mammon Worship' is the prevalent attitude of attaching weight to wealth and of despising poverty. Vast amounts of money are in the hands of wealthy men. To get money, by following human methods, involves going to these wealthy man 'cap in hand' and playing the sycophant. Wealthy people are invited to occupy the best seats in the church building and to fill the important offices in the church. Board members, Board chairmen, Committee members, Committee chairmen, Elders, Deacons, Presidents, Honorary pastors – these seats are largely occupied by people with money. The state of their Faith and the state of their morals are questions not considered. So long as you have money, you can be a church leader. So long as you have money you can occupy the best seats in the church building. So long as you have money you will be respected in the congregation and you will be welcomed even by the pastor. Even when it is known that the wealth of these people has amassed by dealing in opium and trading in tobacco, or by using an official position to squeeze money out of people, or by using other methods that involve others in severe loss to secure their gain – no one takes the trouble to enquire. So long as you can give evidence that you are rich, then no matter where you go you can count on being welcomed and respected. No one will ask whether your wealth has been acquired honestly or not. That is the situation in present-day society; and that is the situation in the present-day church.

This worship of wealth leads to another hateful and shameful practice. It is begging for contributions. In order to carry on the work of God you obviously sometimes require money, but God shows us that what is needed for His work should be offered willingly by those who believe in Him. Only by acting in this way can we please Him (Exodus 25:1,2; Corinthians 9:7). But because the church worships money and neglects the things of God they do not follow the method that He has ordained. What they do instead is to make their appeal obsequiously to the rich.

Poor believers do not have the pastor visit them even once in two years while wealthy believers are visited perhaps two or three times every month. As the saying goes, 'The poor live in the busy market yet no one asks about them while the rich, although living in the depths of the mountains, are seen from afar'. Such a tendency appears even in the churches. How can it do other than cause the name of God to be blasphemed? And how can it do other than cause the weak to stumble?.

An even more hateful practice in some churches is to seek contributions even from unbelievers and evil men, not enquiring whether they worship idols or whether they are atheists.

Is not the God we trust in an omnipotent God? Is not the earth with everything in it subject to His rule? If the church pleases God by the way in which it works for Him can He not provide all that is needed? How can the God who rules heaven and earth allow His servants to go around begging? If God does not provide the money that is needed it means that God is not pleased with the way that the church is working. In that case we had better stop.

2 Conforming to the Pattern of the World
The command which God has given to us is found in

40

Romans 12:2 'Do not be conformed to this world, but be transformed by the renewing of your mind.' In spite of this command the church today is striving to conform to the pattern of the world. The bigger the city in which the church is situated, and the more prestigious the church, then the more does it strive to emulate the world. Let me cite several circumstances in which this conforming to the pattern of the world is evident.

People in secular life who want to promote some enterprise, no matter what it is, show a common tendency. They seek out several men or women of wealth and influence to be a rallying point. They feel that otherwise they will fail to get a hearing from society or to obtain the respect of the people. We frequently see advertisements placed in the newspapers by Middle Schools, Technical Schools and Universities inviting applications from prospective students. Invariably you find an important figure from the military or political sphere to be listed as Chairman of Directors or Honorary Principal. As often as not, however, this Chairman of Directors or honorary Principal has no idea even of the direction in which the main entrance is facing. Even less is revealed of his particular responsibility in the school or of his particular contribution. It is simply that the school authorities urge him to accept this position and almost unconsciously he nods his head. That is all. Where wealthy and influential people are concerned their name alone holds tremendous power of attraction. Small wonder then that people in secular life, no matter what enterprise they are engaged in, will strive to get the support of such people. Cunning people thus make use of a common weakness to advance their own particular enterprise.

Some churches, which are to be pitied, are in this respect conforming to the pattern of the world. They do not preach the Gospel; they do not uplift the Lord Jesus; they do not manifest the good qualities that would appeal to the people who sit in the darkness. Invariably and for no good reason they use the name of some important person such as the head of a government, a manager, or a chairman of some kind, to be a notice board for the church. They hope in this way to enhance the prestige of the church and thus to attract people from outside. Yet it is still an open question whether the personalities they bring forward have yet repented and believed in the Lord Jesus. Even believers should not be used in this way simply on account of their wealth and prestige. How much more serious is it when those exalted by the church have not yet truly believed in Christ! Or who are at best backsliders!

In another matter the church follows the pattern of the world. It is when they invite preachers not on the basis of their faith and zeal and virtue, and knowledge of the way of holiness, but stressing both qualities as natural ability to conduct public relations and manage business. In fact some churches have reached the point at which all they they enquire is from which school or college the applicant graduated. What certificate has he? So long as he has the graduation certificate of a particular university or seminary, that is all that is necessary. Does he believe the Bible or not? Does he believe in Christ's way of salvation or not? Is he truly saved? Is he spiritually minded? What of his manner of life? Is it wholesome? Questions like this are never asked. A candidate may have a firmly held faith. He may live a highly moral life. He may be resolute in his aim to serve God faithfully. He may be clearly called to serve God as well as clearly saved.

But so long as he does not possess the required graduation certificate he cannot expect the people to welcome him.

It is a common feature in schools today that many students are not the least interested in pursuing true knowledge for its own sake. It is only necessary for them to wave a piece of paper – their graduation certificate – and all is well. Society will assure them of an occupation. They will have food to eat. They will be highly respected. We can only lament such untoward circumstances. What happens is that earnest believers who have been truly blessed by God and called to serve Him are given no opportunity to work. On the other hand the important positions in the church are occupied by those who have no other claim than the graduation certificates they clasp in their hand.

There is another deplorable feature in which churches of today are imitating the pattern of the world. It is that many church leaders who influence large groups of believers are actually pursuing the pleasures of sin. Their amusements and habits are 100% of the world. The most grievous aspect is that both leaders and believers are engaged in these things openly. No one reproves them, and they themselves have no feeling of shame. In course of time, therefore, these worldly amusements become accepted as legitimate recreations. The church is thus penetrated and permeated by these detestable practices of the world.

A few years ago in one of our large cities I was confronted with what to me was a most disturbing sight. I had been invited to preach in the chapel and after the bell had rung I went in. Facing us at the back of the platform, and behind the chairs for the pastor and the preacher, was a group of young women. Their clothes were extremely smart – red, green, yellow, purple – and made of dazzling silk. It seemed that no two were wearing the same style. If the people coming in were unaware beforehand that a service of worship was to be held, they would certainly have got the impression, I fear, that it was a fashion show to display beautiful dresses. When you stop to think about it, why in fact were these young women, in their elegant apparel, sitting there on the platform at all? They were of course the choir. But since the function of singing hymns is to praise God why do they have to wear such ornate and eye-catching clothes? I do not blame the young women who were acting in ignorance. But I do want to ask the pastor and the leaders of the church why they look for people like this to make up the choir. And why make them sit on the platform where they face the congregation? And if the church leaders make arrangements like this why is it that no one in the congregation makes a move to protest? Why does no one advocate changing the practice? We know that it is the practice of business firms to employ beautiful and fashionably dressed young women in order to advertise their goods. But what is the real motive of the churches in using such a method? Church leaders ought to be warning believers against conforming to wordly customs like this. Yet not only do the leaders fail to do this, on the contrary they arrange for these young women with their beautiful and alluring dresses to sit prominently on the platform. At the very least it promotes a showy atmosphere; at the most it can indirectly create a path to sin. This is a happening that I have seen not just in one church but in many churches.

God had commanded those who belong to Him to come out from unbelievers and to be separate from them. Yet the church of the present-day persists in

Tares sown by the enemy would grow amongst the wheat

following worldly ways and in going hand in hand with those who are God's enemies. Just as Israel of old disobeyed God's commands and copied the evil ways of Canaan, so does the church of today ignore God's teaching and copy the evil customs of the world.

3 Toleration of Sin

It is not strange that all kinds of sinful practices arise within the bounds of the church, for the Lord Jesus clearly told us that tares sown by the enemy would grow amongst the wheat that He Himself has planted. He also clearly indicated that the wheat referred to His disciples and the tares to those who belong to the devil (Matthew 13:24–30, 36–43). Just as you cannot prevent tares appearing in the wheat field so in the church you cannot prevent the appearance of children of the wicked one. Amongst believers who have truly repented there arise not a few who are carnal and who are easily led into sin. This is not strange. Nor is the situation sufficiently far gone to endanger the church. Nevertheless the church should adopt the attitude of deeply hating sin of any kind and set itself to cut it out, however painful the process may be. Only by acting in this way can the church deliver itself from falling into greater danger. If you follow a policy of tolerating sin and indulging it, then the sinful condition will spread until the church is permeated by it. 'If your brother sins against you, go and tell him his fault between you and him alone. If he hears you, you have gained your brother. But if he will not hear you, then take with you one or two more, that by the mouth of two or three witnesses every word may be established. And if he refuses to hear them, tell it to the church. But if he refuses even to hear the church, let him be to you like a heathen and a tax collector' (Matthew 18:15–17).

These instructions were given to the disciples because the Lord Jesus well knew that the danger arising from tolerating sin was very great. He directed His disciples to exhort the sinning brother in a spirit of love. If he then hardened his heart and refused to repent, if he would not listen to the words either of one brother or of two or three brothers, and if he went further and despised the faithful words of the whole church, all that remains is to treat him as strangers and tax-collectors are treated. This is a safeguard for the whole group of believers.

If on the other hand you refrain from acting according to these instructions then it will become more and more difficult to avoid these evil tendencies being emulated by others in the church. The church will then become permeated by sinful practices.

The apostles also made regulations to deal with the latent danger in the church. You will find references to this issue in the following passages: 1 Corinthians 5:19–23, Galatians 6:1, 2 Thessalonians 3:6, 1 Timothy 5:20, Titus 3:10,11.

The above teaching, which is what the Holy Spirit gave to the church through the apostles, may be summed up as follows. You must approach the one who has sinned in the spirit of meekness and exhort him in the hope that he will repent and change. If he remains obdurate then he should be reproved in front of all concerned. If he still does not respond to rebuke and continues to sin, then the whole church should avoid him, lest others should also be led astray. This exactly tallies with the teaching of the Lord Jesus in the passage quoted earlier.

What is the situation in the church today? Obviously we cannot say that there are no instances of churches that accord with the teaching of the Bible in this respect. But the majority of churches have thrust aside the instruction of Christ and they neither warn nor reprove those who err. Even less do they alert the church as a whole to be on its guard against them.

Look at the list. The covetous, the liars, those who engage in malpractices, those who seek personal gain from public funds, the licentious, those who fail to respect their parents, those who ill-treat their wives, those who drink to excess, those who engage in gambling, and commit sin in many ways – all these and more are found inside the churches. Not only do the churches fail to separate themselves from those who transgress in these ways, they will sometimes appoint these people to positions of authority where they serve as leaders and carry heavy responsibilities. Should they be people of wealth and influence then comment is superfluous. So long as they make substantial contributions to the church, so long as they invite the pastor and other leaders to special meals, and so long as they make a point of handing out presents, no action is taken. In this way a situation arises in which flagrant transgressors are designated 'pillars of the church'. Weak believers are naturally stumbled by these things, and those who have not truly repented become overbearing. Thus the church of Christ is transformed into the den of Satan.

Naturally not all of the corrupted churches have deteriorated to this extent. They do not go as far as appointing wilful transgressors to office. On the other hand they fail to reprimand those who refuse to give up their sin. The reason they tolerate transgressors like this is either through fear of offending them or through not daring to offend them. Again, this is a situation that ought not to be. If you fail to reprimand those who sin wilfully, and make no move to avoid them, evil influences within the church will steadily increase and the church will become thoroughly corrupt.

One thing is hard to understand. The church leaders in these circumstances are not acting to derive personal advantages from these offenders, and at the same time they are acquainted with the teaching of the Scriptures, so why do they still tolerate and indulge these wrongdoers? Why do they not reprove and exhort them, and why do they not charge the whole church to avoid them? As onlookers we can perceive three reasons for this.

The first reason is that church leaders themselves have not a few shortcomings and sinful habits. Since they themselves have been guilty of sinful conduct they have no 'face' to reprove and exhort others who offend. Even if they should ignore 'face' and resort to reproof and exhortation, the offenders will simply ignore them. 'You rebuke us,' they object, 'but ought you not to turn round and rebuke yourselves?'

The second reason is having regard to the general situation. 'Having regard to the general situation' is a very wrong attitude. Many people are fully aware of the things that ought to be done and the things that ought not to be done. They go further and make up their mind to do the things they ought to do and to refrain from doing the things that they ought not to do. But they then have regard to the general situation, and because of this they fail to do what they ought to do and they fail to refrain from the things that they ought not to do. This is one cause of the lowering of moral standards. It is one cause of the failure to eliminate evil practices in society. 'Having regard to the general situation' has ruined many projects and brought harm to I don't know how many people. through having regard to the general situation many believers inside the church have fallen into sin and no one has been willing to rebuke them and exhort them. Even less is anyone willing to urge believers to keep away from people who persist in their sin. Thus does the evil spread, until the whole church is contaminated.

The third reason is fear of persecution. To speak to people about their faults is far from easy. To add reproof to exhortation is even more difficult. To urge the whole church to avoid those who stubbornly refuse to repent is something more difficult still. Those who are prepared to go as far as this can hardly avoid giving offence and thus incurring persecution. Many believers are unwilling to take this risk, and church leaders will go out of their way to avoid it. So the situation in the church continues to deteriorate.

To sum up, it is essential that the whole church change its direction and obey the teaching of the Lord Jesus, and that the church follows the rules set up for the church by the Holy Spirit and communicated through the apostles.

I have observed, in various churches, a most detestable state of affairs. There have been people of evil character who were involved in practising evil. Yet not only did no one reprove or exhort them, nor make any move to compel them to leave the church, but on the contrary they were shielded and favoured. If it were a case of church leaders being unaware of the situation this attitude would not be strange. What makes it strange is that even when these evil-doings are exposed the church leaders still remain aloof. This may be because those involved are friends or relatives of the leaders. Should anyone get up to admonish those involved then the church leaders can still cover-up for them and defend them. The sin of the church leaders in these circumstances is far greater than that of the original offenders.

7.
Being both a
lion and a lamb...

Revelation 5: 1–7

The apostle John once had a vision of God holding in His hand a scroll that was sealed with seven seals. But no one was able to open the scroll, so he wept. Then an elder spoke to him, saying, 'Behold, the lion of the tribe of Judah, the Root of David, has prevailed to open the scroll and to loose its seven seals.' Immediately after that, John saw the Lamb take the scroll out of the hand of God.

All who read that passage will understand that 'the Lion of the tribe of Judah' and the Lamb looking 'as it had been slain' both have reference to the Lord Jesus. How strange! The lion and the lamb are animals totally unlike each other. The lion is one of the fiercest among the wild beasts while the lamb among the anaimals is one of the mildest. The lion is capable of subduing other beasts but none of the other beasts can subdue the lion. The lamb is completely different. Not only is it incapable of subduing other animals it is itself at their mercy. It has no strength to resist; it is not in its nature to resist; and on no account will it attempt to do so. So it can be dragged to a place of slaughter without it making the slightest effort to resist.

Since these two animals are totally different from each other how is it that the Bible calls the Lord Jesus a lion and at the same time refers to Him as a lamb? If He is a lion, how can He be a lamb? And if He is a lamb, how can He be a lion? The fact remains that in this passage of the Bible He is described in these two ways. What is the explanation?

The lion and the lamb represent different periods. When our Lord Jesus first came into the world He came as a lamb. Take note how meek and lowly and gentle and humble He was at that time. 'When He was reviled (He) did not revile in return, when He suffered, He did not threaten, but committed Himself to Him who judges righteously – by whose stripes you were healed' (1 Peter 2: 23).

Anyone could take advantage of Him. Anyone could ill-treat Him. Yet He strove with no one. 'He was oppressed, and he was afflicted, yet he opened not his mouth; he was led as a lamb to the slaughter, and as a sheep before its shearers is dumb, so he opened not his mouth' (Isaiah 53: 7).

But when He comes the second time He will be the universal ruler. He will come in glory and majesty like a lion. 'God will give Him the heathen for His inheritance and the uttermost parts of the earth for His possession. He shall break them with a rod of iron

Being both a lion and a lamb

and dash them in pieces like a potter's vessel'. (Psalm 2: 8,9).

Yet even when our Lord came into the world the first time He wasn't always meek like a lamb; sometimes He exercises majestic and fearsome power like a lion. If we study the Gospel records carefully we shall discover that whenever He was insulted and derided, or when He was subjected to invective and persecution, He was invariably meek and gentle like a lamb. But whenever He was stirred to righteous anger, as when the issue was the truth and righteousness of God, He was firece and fearful like a lion. See Him for instance in the temple. Was He not majestic and fearful like a lion? Listen to Him reproving the scribes and Pharisees: 'Woe to you, scribes and Pharisees, hyprocrites! For you cleanse the outside of the cup and the dish, but inside they are full of extortion and self-indulgence. Blind Pharisees, first cleanse the inside of the cup and dish, that the outside of them may be clean also' (Matthew 23: 25–28).

These scribes and Pharisees held position and power in Jewish society. They were everywhere esteemed and respected. Yet it was without regard for their feelings that the Lord uncovered their plotting and rebuked their sin. Was He not forceful and fierce like a lion?

Whenever He was insulted or ill-treated He was as gentle as a lamb. But whenever He fought for truth and righteousness He was as vigorous and forceful as a lion. In that way our Lord was both Lamb and Lion.

What about us who are disciples of the Lord? Ought we not to be like Him in these things? That is, when we are insulted, opposed, or persecuted; or when we suffer injury; ought we not to be gentle like a lamb and on no account strive with our adversaries? However, when we are witnessing to our Faith and to the Truth of God ought we not to be forceful and fierce like a lion? No matter how men threaten or intimidate us, and no matter what misfortunes or dangers confront us, we must confess the name of the Lord without fail. Our hearts must be set to follow the way of the Lord and on no account to rebel against His commands. We must fear neither threats nor difficulty nor danger. We should press ahead like lions with no thought whatever of retreating. We may be feared – but we shall not fear. A good Christian should never strive with anyone on account of money, property, possessions or fame. But at the same time he should never yield an inch when it is a matter of Faith and Truth. When it is appropriate to act like a lamb he should act like a lamb; but when it is appropriate to act like a lion he should act like a lion.

We acknowledge that there are certainly many Christians who resemble both lion and lamb. But unhappily the occasions when they act like the lion or the lamb are inappropriate. When they ought to act like a lion, they act like a lamb. And when they ought to act like a lamb, they act like a lion. At a time when they ought to be boldly fighting for the Faith and for the Truth they are as soft as water. They keep their mouths closed and they utter no word. They may even reach the point at which, in order to avoid opposition and suffering, they follow the path of unbelievers and participate in many activities that are contrary to the truth. On the other hand, if anyone should put in jeopardy their property, their business, their profits or their reputation, they are unwilling to yield to them in the slightest and, immediately stiffening themselves, they confront those who would take advantage of them without hesitation. Obverve the attitude of Christian people when they are in dispute with people over money, property, reputation or possessions – many of them are stern and ruthless in the extreme, just like harsh and frightening lions. Yet at a time when they should be making a stand on account of Faith and Truth they become meek and gentle like a lamb with nothing to say whatever. Compare people who act in this way with the example that was set by our Lord and you will want to weep.

This painful and shameful phenomenon is one that shows itself everywhere. When matters of property and possessions are at issue in the home you will find fierce quarrels arising between husband and wife, between brothers and sisters, and even between children and parents. Relatives turn into thieves and become enemies; brothers act among themselves as if at war. People in society, in order to grab land and power and in order to amass wealth, will curse each other and fight each other and go to law with each other and even kill each other. While originally they were relatives and neighbours, co-operating like friends, eventually in the interests of paltry gain and power they become enemies. No longer can they associate together. Every man regards his money, his reputation and his property as a priceless treasure on which there must on no account be any infringement. They reach the point at which truth and righteousness no longer have any value on their thinking. No one is prepared to fight for such qualities. It is painful enough to see people of the world who act in this way, but contrary to expectation you not infrequently find Christian people also who act in this way. What can be more lamentable than this?

When a Christian clashes with other people and quarrels with them on account of his possessions, wealth, property, reptuation, authority or estate he should be ashamed of himself. For he is not acting like His Lord. He throws away his standing as a saint. When a Christian clashes with other people in matters like this and asks me to help him settle the affair, without having to investigate I consider him to be not a good Christian. For if he is oppressing others he obviously has no ground to stand on. And if it is a case of him being oppressed and he wants to offer resistance, then again he is unlike his Lord. At the same time if a Christian dare not make a stand in order to maintain the Faith and the Truth of God it becomes a matter of shame. For he is not emulating his Lord and he forfeits his role as a saint.

Let us quickly acknowledge our failures and errors

of the past. We must ask God to have mercy upon us so that from now on we refrain from striving with men for our own gain or glory. At the same time we should ask the Lord to give us courage so that when it comes to matters of the Faith and of Truth we do not yield even an inch. Our Lord is both a Lamb and a Lion. We also ought to be both a lamb and a lion in the same way that He is.

8.
Accepting God's will...

Mark 6: 31; John 13: 6,7

The Lord Jesus Christ had compassions on the multitude when He saw their need. He was also conscious of the strain His disciples were under when they were hard-pressed. On one occasion He said to them, 'Come aside by yourselves to a deserted place and rest awhile'. The Scripture goes on, 'For there was much coming and going, and they did not have time to eat. And they departed into a desert place by ship privately.' But they were pursued by the people, and were denied the rest they so badly needed.

This is sometimes the case with God's people. They have a need, and it is a real need. It looks as though it is being supplied but then it is strangely denied them. There was an occasion when the Lord Jesus Christ washed the feet of Simon Peter and Peter said to Him, 'Lord, are you washing my feet?' Jesus answered and said unto him, 'What I am doing you do not understand now; but you will know after this.' It was strange behaviour to Peter, and he was not to know the reason for it, but he would know later. He must trust the Lord Jesus until then.

Dear Christian, chosen by and beloved of the Lord, you should trust the Lord without the slightest shadow of doubt, uneasiness or fear. The Lord loves you, once died for you, redeemed you and has made you his heir. Since the Lord loves you so, He will never do anything that is detrimental to you. Admittedly, some of the things that the Lord ordained to happen to you might apparently be your loss, your grief, and might puzzle and perplex you. But if you remember that Jesus said, 'What I am doing you do not understand now; but you will know after this,' you will be greatly comforted and gladdened. Sometimes you are really made to suffer for no apparent reason. You really don't know why it happened to you: you haven't done anything wrong, nor have you been indiscreet or incompetent to merit this evil. At such times you might perhaps want to reproach the Lord for not protecting you, for letting you suffer such losses. Perhaps you even begin to throw doubts on the Lord's love, authority and power because of this. At such times, please remember that the Lord said, 'What I am doing you will not understand now; but you will know after this.'

Sometimes people misunderstand you and suddenly turn against you. You become downcast and even broken-hearted. You wonder why the Lord allows this to happen, why He doesn't clear such misunderstandings for you, why loving you as He does He does not deliver you from the people who are against you. At such times, please think about the Lord's words, 'What I am doing you do not understand now; but you will know after this.'

Sometimes, someone dearly loved is suddenly taken away from you. Your heart seems to have been taken away also. You feel as though you have lost everything. You grumble that the Lord has treated you too cruelly. You feel that it would have been far easier to bear if the Lord had asked you to sustain any loss other than this. You feel that the Lord has deliberately made you to bear the one thing that is most difficult to bear. At such times I beg of you to meditate on the Lord's words, 'What I am doing you do not understand now; but you will know after this.'

Sometimes you fall sick and stay in bed with pain, but without any indication of a cure. You might well feel depressed and miserable. You ask in your heart, 'What is the meaning of this?' 'Were I in good health could I not serve the Lord and help other people?' 'Why does the Lord want me to waste so much precious time in bed so that in addition to being unable to work I have to endure the misery of illness?' At such times please do not ask any more such pointless questions. You need only believe what the Lord said, 'What I am doing you do not understand now; but you will know after this.'

Sometimes you might accidentally hurt yourself and so damage a member of your body, your eye, or ear, or hand, or foot or another part of the body. Your sorrow and frustration then beggar description. You feel that the joy of this life is henceforth lost to you and that there is no more hope for achieving those things that you have set out to do. Your heart is filled with darkness and affliction. At such times you need to ponder over the Lord's words, 'What I am doing you do not understand now; but you will know after this.'

Sometimes you are sorely tried for many a day and cannot run away from it, though you have tried again and again to get away. Unfortunately, there is no escape. Many a time you wish to know why the Lord wants you to be tried for such a long time. Neither could you see how such trials could be of any benefit to you. You begin to lose heart and to yield because the contest is so long drawn out. At such times, please continue to believe on the Lord's words, 'What I am doing you do not understand now; but you will know after this.'

No matter what sorrows, sufferings or disasters befall you, do not lose heart. He can never be wrong. What He does is for your good. Oftentimes, He makes you sustain a little loss, purely to make you gain a lot. To taste a little temporary bitterness in order to make you have everlasting satisfaction. You can only see the things now in front of you, you cannot perceive the distant future. But the Lord had His whole plan made long ago. Whatever might befall you, you should trust the Lord with singleness of heart, wait on the Lord and patiently endure all the tribulations and bear in mind always the Lord's words, 'What I am doing you do not understand now; but you will know after this.'

9.
One who practised free love...

Judges 14: 1–3

'Now Samson went down to Timnath, and saw a woman in Timnath of the daughters of the Philistines.

So he went up, and told his father and his mother, saying, I have seen a woman in Timnath of the daughters of the Philistines: now therefore get her for me as a wife'.

Then his father and his mother said unto him, 'Is there no woman among the daughters of your brethren, or among all my peoople, that you must go and get a wife from uncircumcised Philistines?' and Samson said unto his father, 'Get her for me, for she pleases me well.'

Judges 14: 7
'Then he went down, and talked with the woman; and she pleased Samson well.'

Judges 16: 1
'Then went Samson to Gaza, and saw a prostitute there, and went in to her.'

Judges 16: 4
'Now afterwards it happened that he loved a woman in the valley of Sorek, whose name was Delilah.'

During the past few years a large number of young people have advocated the practice of free love. In their view the people of past generations did not understand the meaning of 'free love', and they did not therefore enjoy the pleasures of free love. Those who hold this view, however, do not realise that several thousand years ago there were already people who practised free love. For instance there are passages in ancient Chinese books that tell of young people practising free love. The Bible, also, narrates the history of one who practised free love – and this was a man who had been the instrument of God. He was a warrior specially raised up by God to deliver the people of Israel from the hand of the Philistines. His name was Samson.

In the above three passages of Scripture we observe how he encountered three women in three different places, and how he practised free love with each of them. On the first occasion he met a Philistine woman in Timnah. He fell for her as soon as he met her and wanted to take her as his wife. It was not because she was virtuous; it was not because she was clever; nor was it because she was good at managing a home. It was simply because she pleased him. This is exactly the reason advanced by certain young people today who advocate free love. They see no need to enquire about the respective families of the partners. They do not see the need to enquire into their level of intelligence. Even less do they see the need to enquire about character. All that is necessary, in their view, is 'to see her and to fall in love with her'. That is all that is necessary to practise free love. Since this kind of love is free, no one has authority to ask questions and even less has anyone authority to stand in the way. In the interests of free love one can sacrifice one's business; in the interests of free love one can sacrifice one's future; in the interests of free love one can sacrifice one's home; and in the interests of free love one can sacrifice one's parents. All one needs to say is, 'She pleases me', and there is nothing more to be said.

Although Samson had previously been obstructed in this by his parents, he did not on this account hesitate. He overcame all obstacles. 'Then he went down, and talked with the woman; and she pleased Samson well.' However, after only a few days, because the woman he loved had divulged the secret of his riddle, and caused him to lose face in the presence of his friend, he was very angry and went up to his father's house. The marriage had not been built on a sound foundation; Samson had not considered whether it was in every way suitable. Before they came together both he and his wife had been subject to passion, so their eyes were closed and neither could see the shortcomings of the other. But as soon as their passions subsided they became aware of each other's shortcomings. Thus it only required a few trivial incidents and a few trivial utterances to bring about a major rift. The woman of Timnath cheated Samson, forcing him to tell her the meaning of the riddle. Then

Samson became very angry with her and he separated from her and returned to his own home. Unless marriage is built on a firm foundation, and not dependent on passing emotions, it rarely lasts. The type of situation depicted here is multiplied in our own day beyond reckoning. 'Free love! Free love!' How many tragedies are enacted today in the name of free love! How many young men and women have been permanently scarred?

After a while Samson again thought about his wife. He took with him the kid of a goat and visited her. But he was staggered to find that she already had another lover. His father-in-law said to him:'I really thought that you thoroughly hated her. Therefore I gave her to your companion. Is not her younger sister better than she? Please take her instead.' Not only was it Samson who looked upon marriage as a game, his father-in-law did also. Although Samson in his anger over what had happened had gone away, the woman was still married to him. But her father was intolerant of the situation and in a very short time he gave his daughter to someone else. How can we challenge the conclusion that this had happened because the woman was accustomed to practising free love? When Samson was not at hand she had fallen in love with his companion. The husband did not act like a husband; the wife did not act like a wife; and the father-in-law did not act like a father-in-law. It was a case of ingoring the customary rules and giving rein to passion; such were the habits of those who advocated free love.

Calamity soon followed. In his anger Samson used foxes and torches to burn the Philistines' crops and olive groves. The Philistines could not handle Samson so they vented their anger on his father-in-law and his family. They 'burnt her and her father with fire'.

Samson also took revenge on the Philistines, smiting them with a great slaughter. The comedy was thus transformed into an ugly drama; changing further it became a tragedy of mutual revenge and killing. What a frightening story of free love!

No matter how much Samson became angry; no matter how much he took revenge; his lover was already dead and would not live again. He had to go and search for another lover. He continued to practise free love and on this second occasion the one whom he found was worse than the first. It was a harlot. In the words of Scripture, 'Then went Samson to Gaza, and saw a prostitute there, and went in to her.' So it is with many who practise free love. This is not really love. All it means for them is a desire to approach one of the opposite sex and to indulge their passions. They make no enquiry as to the virtue or integrity or knowledge or ability of the one they approach; it is sufficient if they find one who is beautiful and handsome and romantic, so that they can indulge their passions. If the partner is a harlot it does not matter.

People like this are injurious to society. When a person who originally had faith and ambition and hope and virtue gets in with people like this he or she will sooner or later become confused and lose his own faith and ambition and hope and virtue. That is what happened to Samson. Although he was chosen by God he got so mixed up that he finished down and out. His life was dominated not by love but by hatred. Samson is surely the clearest possible warning to us.

Before long Samson was involved with yet another woman. This time it was Delilah. So far as we can see, she was Samson's third lover. In our own day those who talk about free love are in the same category as Samson. In the space of a few years they are guilty of changing their lover several times. A couple today may be lovers; but tomorrow they become enemies. Their modesty, their moral rectitude, and their credibility are completely swept away. At one stage two people cannot be more bound up with each other; but before long they are reduced to reviling and insulting each other.

Some think nothing of seducing the wife of a friend or a colleague. They are 'so used to seeing those who are beautiful that it means nothing to them'. Even more shameful is when those of an older generation seduce their relatives in a younger generation. Sometimes a man will go so far as to urge a woman amongst them to leave her husband and to throw in her lot with him. Or he may take advantage of a woman's husband being in sick-bed or in prison to get the wife into his own hands. There are also cases of school principals who abandon their wives in order to have immoral relations with their students. They accomplish this under cover of extra classes with high sounding names like appreciation of music and advanced lesson in painting. Cases of this are too numerous to reckon. Some who live together having dispensed with a wedding ceremony often suffer a change of mood and this results in 'a temporary dissolution of partnership'. Marriage is essentially a sacred and honourable institution; how grievous that the advocates of free love should regard it as something objectionable!

What was it that lay behind the free love as practised by Samson and Delilah? Samson was enamoured of the beauty of Delilah while Delilah coveted the wealth of the Philistines. The leaders of the Philistines pleaded with Delilah to deceive Samson and to find out for them the secret of his great strength. 'And the lords of the Philistines came up to her, and said to her, Entice him, and find out where his great strength lies, and by what means we may overpower him, that we may bind him to afflict him; and everyone of us will give you eleven hundred pieces of silver.'

In that way one who had triumphed valiantly over an army of a thousand now meekly handed himself over to an agent of the enemy and allowed her to do with him what she wanted. Could anything be more stupid? When we read this point we break out in sweat on Samson's account just to think of it. Yet what was Samson doing? He still regarded himself as enjoying a most pleasant life – it was like being a swallow amid the burning roof of a house and like a fish swimming in a cauldron. What a perilous situation! Yet Samson still seemed unaware of it.

We find, alas, the same situation today. For the position of many young men and women who practise free love is just like that. Men are infatuated by women's beauty and women are covetous of men's estate. Or it may be the reverse. But those who are enamoured of beauty one day come across someone who has even greater beauty and it is not long before they experience a change of heart. And when those who aspire after property discover that their partner does not possess property their attitude soon changes to disdain (lit. turn the whites of the eyes upon). When both sides are corrupted and when each is using the other there is a rough balance of power.

Most tragic of all is when one partner has genuine affection while the affection of the other partner is merely a pretence. So you must choose your partner with great care. When you are hiring a servant, even though you only want him to do various jobs for you around the house, you still enquire before you engage him whether he is reliable. You also require him to provide a guarantor. When you get married you purpose to commit to your partner your life and your home and your possessions – and indeed your happiness – so how can you enter into it lightly and take fewer precautions than when you engage a servant? It would be a foolish and hazardous thing to do. Yet there are many young men and women who happen to meet someone of the opposite sex and without knowing her (or him) very much they go ahead and get engaged and married without any foundation to the marriage other than mutual sensual attraction. Small wonder that many of these marriages deteriorate and end up in the partners separating.

In Samson's case it was not long before he tasted the bitter fruit of his love affairs. His lover Delilah coveted the wealth of the Philistines who sought by one means or another to discover the source of his strength. Samson fully realised that his lover was planning to take advantage of him and that is why he answered her three times with lies. On the first occasion he said, 'If they bind me with seven fresh bowstrings, not yet dried, then shall I become weak, and be like any other man.' On the second occasion he said, 'If they bind be securely with new ropes that have never been used, then shall I be weak, and be like any other man.' On the third occasion he said, 'If you weave the seven locks of my head into the web of the loom'. Three times he responded with lies and three times Delilah was deceived. Finally Delilah used the kind of method that a woman can use with a man. She said, 'How can you say, I love thee, when your heart is not with me?' Moreover, 'she pestered him daily with her words, and pressed him, so that his soul was vexed unto death.' From these two passages we can conclude that she was constantly talking with

Samson about love. Samson for his part must have told her repeatedly how he loved her. So she took him up on his declarations and argued, 'How can you say, I love thee, when your heart is not with me?' All this time she was scheming to betray Samson. Yet Samson knew all the time that Delilah was not to be trusted. This is obvious from the fact that he repeatedly told lies to evade the issue. He steeled himself not to reveal the secret of his strength. From the fact that Samson's soul was vexed unto death when she pressed him daily we can see even more clearly that Samson was fully aware of Delilah's artful devices. He knew perfectly well that if he told her the truth, it could lead to disaster. Since this was so, why did not Samson keep right away from this 'powerful enemy bed-fellow'? It was partly because Samson was enamoured of her beauty and also because Delilah was able to delude Samson with her wiles. It is plain for all to see that Delilah was certainly a fascinating and seductive and deceiving woman who was able to employ soft words and honeyed speech to bring pressure on a man. Women like this have no idea of the meaning of love and affection that is genuine and sincere. When they talk to men about sensual love the reason is either to satisfy their own lusts or else it is to gain some benefit.

Of course, many men are only too willing to associate with women like this, and to take them as wives, since it brings them some measure of sensual satisfaction. But the only satisfactory course is to keep right away from such women. For once you approach them you are liable to be betrayed. And you may find yourself unable to break away.

How then can you escape from misfortunes like this? It is necessary that you watch yourself from the beginning, and whenever you come across women of

You must avoid these women as you avoid wild animals

this nature you must avoid them as you avoid wild animals. The same is to be said of men for there are men with the same fierce disposition. The men rely on the appeal of money and vain glory, on soft words and honeyed speech, to lead ignorant women astray. On the surface they simply talk about love but actually they simply want women in order to satisfy their lusts. And women of limited vision are easily deceived by them. They accept all that the men say as being true. They think that everything is as it appears on the surface. They are deluded into thinking that by marrying men like this they can enter a realm of happiness. No matter how other people warn them and try to stop them, they simply close their ears and refuse to listen. In fact they suspect these well-wishers of trying to spoil their love affairs and to rob them of their happiness. So they react strongly. If their friends continue to exhort them, they break off relations with them. If their parents put pressure on them, they leave home. So they are ensnared in the net. But sooner or later, in all probability, those heartless men abandon them and they are left in misery. One day the women awake and repent of their previous errors. But the die has been cast and there is no way to restore the situation.

In the Bible we have this record of one man, Samson, who suffered great misfortune as a result of practising free love. But what is the situation today? There are now innumerable young men and women who travel the same path as Samson. I only wish I could get hold of each one of them and tell them the story of Samson.

No matter how unwilling Samson was to reveal the source of his strength, he was unable to resist Delilah's importunity. 'She pressed him daily with her words, and urged him . . .' No matter how strong a man is, he cannot resist the steady pressure of a woman. Many men are well aware that they ought to heed the words of their parents, but because their wives press them daily with their words, their attitude to their parents undergoes a change. Many men are well aware that they ought to love their brothers, but because their wives press them daily with their words, they regard even their brothers as enemies. Many men are well aware that they ought to be upright and free from corruption, but because their wives press them daily with their words they begin to engage in malpractices. Many men are well aware that they ought to maintain good relations with their neighbours, but because their wives press them daily with their words they allow friction to arise.

Because of pressure from their wives, many men become stubborn and undutiful. Because of pressure from their wives, many officials become avaricious. Because of pressure from their wives, some men have ended up in prison. Some have committed murder. Thus innumerable men have fallen into sin and brought misery on themselves because of their wives bringing pressure on them with their words. Once a man grasps the potential consequences of an unsuitable union could he again regard love and marriage as trifling matters?

Because Samson could not sustain the pressure he finally capitulated and told Delilah what he ought not to have told her. 'He told her all his heart, and said to her, no razor has ever come upon my head; for I have been a Nazarite unto God from my mother's womb: if I am shaven, then my strength will leave me, and I shall become weak, and be like any other man.' That's it! That's it! Samson was finished! He had revealed to Delilah what he ought on no account to have revealed. Not only did he injure himself, he also injured the Israelites. He also dishonoured the name of God. Here was a warrior of unprecedented strength who had been raised up by God, yet he was utterly humiliated at the hands of a woman who had given herself as an instrument to his enemies. Simply to think of it makes one tremble.

'And when Delilah saw that he had told her with all his heart, she sent and called for the lords of the Philistines, saying, Come up this once more for he hath told me all his heart. So the lords of the Philistines came up to her, and brought the money in their hand.

'And she lulled him to sleep upon her knees; and

called for a man, and had him to shave off the seven locks of his head; and she began to torment him, and his strength left him.

'And she said, The Philistines are upon thee, Samson. So he awoke from his sleep and said, I will go out as before at other times and shake myself free. But he did not know that the Lord had departed from him.

'Then the Philistines took him, and put out his eyes, and brought him down to Gaza. They bound him with bronze fetters and he became a grinder in the prison.'

What a fearful woman was Delilah! What a stupid person was Samson! Delilah never ceased her efforts to discover the source of Samson's strength in order that she might ruin him. And she attained her objective. Samson clearly knew that Delilah could not be trusted, but in the end he failed to escape from her snares and he told her his secret. The leaders of the Philistines had already arrived and were waiting by him ready to lay hold of him. Delilah on her part had arranged for a man to cut off Samson's hair while he was asleep on her lap.

That group of watchers was just like a band of hunters who had already dug a pit and who were waiting with their weapons to capture a lion. The lion was making its way towards the pit seemingly quite unconscious of danger. And thus it has been all down the years. Countless warriors of God have at first been greatly used by Him but one day they allowed their passions to carry them away and they have then found themselves in the hand of Satan. Love and affection are the gifts of God. They are good gifts and we do not oppose them. But lust and licentiousness are both dangerous and frightening. Many men and women have overcome Satan in every conceivable respect except in this matter of the opposite sex. They go to sleep, as it were, on Delilah's lap. And that is where they fall into the hands of Satan.

The predicament of Samson after he had fallen into the hands of the Philistines was truly pitiful. They 'put out his eyes, and brought him down to Gaza, they bound him with bronze fetters; and he became a grinder in the prison.' Most of the sins of lust and licentiousness arise through the eyes, and it was Samson's eyes that were destroyed by the enemy so that even the ordinary things open to the sight of other people were hidden from him. It is the same with many people today. As a result of their sins they suffer the loss of health and even life. Even those blessings that God would give them they are no longer able to enjoy. As Samson had to grind wheat for the enemy, so do transgressors today have to suffer bitterness at the hands of the enemy.

Here was a warrior who had once been a match for a thousand men, yet he came to a pitiful end in this way simply because he gave rein to his lusts. Samson was not brought to nothing by the Philistines; nor by Delilah; it was by Samson himself. Had Samson not been promiscuous in the way he was, then let there be thousands of Delilahs out to harm him, and let the whole army of the Philistines plot to seize him, he would still have overcome them. But simply because he could not control himself, it was possible for a single Delilah together with a small detachement of Philistines to subdue him totally. How frightening is the power of sin and sensuality!

We do not know how many tens of thousands of Israelites there were at the time of Samson, but what the Philistines brooded over for a long time was how to get hold of just one of them – Samson. They well knew that no one else among the Israelites was capable of achieving anything great, and that only this valiant Samson was really worth attacking. So long as Samson was around they could not feel secure. As a consequence all the Philistines awaited an opportunity to deal with him. Had Samson grasped this fact even imperfectly he would have realised that he should pass his days in fear and trembling; that he should keep a tight rein on himself; and that both for the honour of God and for the sake of Israel he should take precautions against the plotting of the Philistines. He was a young man. He had the right to exercise his love and affection. He had the right to marry a wife. But he ought to have married an Israelite woman of high moral standing and one who could be trusted. Had he done so he would certainly have been Israel's defender throughout his life. And the ambitious Philistines would not have been able to encroach even one step on their territory. Nor would Samson have forfeited his standing as a warrior, unique among warriors, who was always able to finsih what he had begun. Unhappily he gave rein to his lusts and fell for any woman he happened to meet. His mind ws taken up with the practice of free love; he neglected the responsibilities which were his and ignored the dangers that always threatened. As a consequence he fell into the hands of the enemy and thus allowed the Philistines to carry out their purposes. The end result was that the Israelites were greatly afflicted (lit. to be amid mire and coals) and that his own life ended in disaster.

Is there not a comparable situation today in that Satan still pays particular attention to those who are chosen by God for special ministry? Those are the ones whom he particularly wants to ensnare – those who have outstanding power and gifts, and who are being used by God in a striking way. Satan is well aware that to capture a believer like this may be greater in its effects than capturing thousands of ordinary believers. As the ancient saying has it, 'When capturing rebels, first secure the leader.'

Satan clearly appreciates the logic of this. Daily therefore he looks for opportunities to disrupt the activities of men and women with special gifts and special influence. Moreover, Satan has many potential instruments with which to achieve his objective. Amongst these instruments are wealth, vainglory, and involvement with the oppoisite sex. For a believer to overcome the temptation of money is certainly not easy; to overcome the temptation of vainglory is also difficult; but to overcome the temptation posed by involvement with the opposite sex is more difficult than either of the other two. As the saying has it: 'It is hard for heroes to overcome the crisis of a pretty woman'. When we appreciate this danger we shall be particularly careful in matters of love and marriage.

Men and women not yet married must not treat this matter lightly; they should regard marriage as a matter of supreme importance. For your marriage has a strong bearing on your life's success or failure, bringing happiness or woe. It also has a strong bearing on the revival or decline of the church. You should make marriage a matter of earnest prayer, asking God to guide you so that you never take even one step astray. Believers who are already married ought to watch themselves in the same way. If your partner is one who worships God and who can help you in the development of your spiritual life then you should listen to his or her exhortation. But if your partner is one who does not worship God – self-centred, cruel, a lover of vainglory, jealous – you must not follow her (or him). At the same time you must not allow hate to seep in either. You must watch yourself continually lest Satan uses her (or him) to take you captive. For while not a few men have suffered harm through putting their trust in dissolute women, the number of saints who have stumbled through the influence of ungodly wives is even greater. A 'desert Delilah' is naturally frightening, but a 'domestic Delilah' has far greater potentiality for inflicting spiritual damage on her husband. For in the eyes of the husband a 'domestic Delilah' is not reckoned a Delilah but as the virtuous wife who will help him to be successful and get rich. So believers lose thier spiritual vision and their spiritual power. They are no longer in a position to fight as God's warriors. Like Samson they end up in confinement, and they are reduced to working for Satan.

In the pages of the Bible there is only *one* Samson. But today there are thousands of Samsons. In the time of Samson the Philistines sought on Delilah to serve as their instrument. What Satan is seeking in the world today is not *one* Delilah but thousands of Delilahs.

10.
The light of the world...

John 8: 12; Matthew 5: 14–16

How strange! On the one hand Jesus said, '*I* am the light of the world!' On the other hand He said, '*You* are the light of the world!'

When the Lord Jesus stated that He was the light of the world, He spoke the truth. For that is exactly what He was. The world had been full of darkness, but it was only necessary for the Lord Jesus to come and immediately the light was made manifest. For several thousand years mankind had been groping in the darkness. Men were ignorant of God's might; they were ignorant of His splendour; and they were ignorant of His compassion. They were also unaware of their own uncleanness; of their own wickedness;

and of their own wretchedness and poverty. The path of life that men should follow and the duties that they should perform were alike beyond their understanding. Nor could they discern men's destiny. The deceptions of the devil, and the pitfalls and snares that he had set, were likewise hidden from their sight.

But as soon as the Lord Jesus came into the world all was changed. God now became knowable. Men could now perceive His might; they could now perceive His splendour; they could now perceive His holiness; and they could now perceive His compassion. Throughout the thirty years that Jesus lived on earth He consistently manifested God to the people around Him. The miracles that He performed served to demonstrate God's might. The teaching that He gave portrayed God's splendour. And the noble life He lived expressed God's holiness. Wherever Jesus went His acts were marked by compassion. He helped people; He forgave people; He healed people; He comforted people; and He delivered people. Finally He was crucified for men's sin. In all these ways He clearly demonstrated that God was a God of compassion. When Philip said to Him, 'Lord, show us the Father', Jesus replied, 'Have I been with you so long, and yet you have not known me, Philip? He who has seen me has seen the Father.'

But there is another aspect. When Jesus was on earth He spoke plainly and reproved men for their sins. He brought it home to them that all their pretence and all their deceitfulness, all their greed and all their self-seeking, all their envy and all their hatred, all their indulgence and all their licentiousness, all their blasphemy and all their reviling, all their pride and all their arrogance – all these things were shameful and detestable. Jesus brought it home to men that not only their wicked ways but also their unrighteous words and unclean thoughts, in the eyes of God, were all evil. By His own holy and blameless life He did two things. On the one hand He exposed the depravity of the people. On the other hand through His teaching and preaching, and through all that He did – culminating in His glorious resurrection – He showed men the path that they should follow and the duties that they should perform. He also revealed the hope and end of life.

In addition to this Jesus threw light on the machinations of the devil; He showed up the pitfalls and snares set by Satan. Jesus was the light. He 'was the true light which gives light to every man who comes into the world' (John 1: 9). It would be natural and reasonable for mankind to love this light and to welcome it. But contrary to expectation, 'men loved darkness rather than light, because their deeds were evil. For every one who does evil hates the light and does not come to the light, lest his deeds should be exposed' (John 3: 19,20). Thieves and robbers who operate at night are no lovers of the light. And it is for a similar reason that evil-doers are consumed with hatred for 'the light of the world'. Men were hostile to Jesus; they turned their back on Him; and they condemned Him. They finally crucified Him on a cross of wood.

But the fact that men hated the light did not in the slightest deflect Jesus from His mission. His sense of responsibility as the light of the world never weakened. Listen to what Jesus said! 'As long as I am in the world, I am the light of the world' (John 9: 5). What He said was true. So long as He was on earth, no day passed without Him shedding His light; no place did He visit without carrying the light.

But Jesus is no longer in the world. After He had

risen from the dead, and after He had companied with His disciples for a number of days, He ascended to the heavens to be seated at God's right hand. He now awaits the day ordained by God when He shall come to the world once again. When that day comes a great light will shine over all the earth, and all will see His glory. But what about the period between His ascension to heaven and His coming again to earth? So long as He was in the world He was the light of the world. But now that He is not in the world, who will take His place and become the light of the world? This matter was already in His mind and He had already made preparation. He raised up certain people to whom He said, 'You are the light of the world!' Who are these people? Can it be other than those of us who are His disciples?

What a marvellous mandate! What a noble calling! What an exalted position! Inasmuch as our Lord said, on the one hand, 'I am the light of the world', and on the other hand, 'You are the light of the world', He places us on the same level as Himself. He raises our standing so that we become honoured like Himself. He takes the commission that He Himself has borne and places it on our shoulders. He takes the work that He Himself has carried on in the world and entrusts it to us. Truly it should cause us 'to receive favour and to be in awe', and to be so moved by gratitude that though 'words fail the tears fall'. Surely we should respond loyally and be 'bursting with enthusiasm'.

We who were wicked and unrighteous are the recipients of His compassion and cleansing and deliverance and redemption. This alone is wonderful beyond all imagination. How much more wonderful is it that He should regard us so highly that He raises us up to be 'the light of the world' in the same way that He Himself was the light of the world. What a glorious privilege!

Since we are to be 'the light of the world' in the same way that He was 'the light of the world', then our words and deeds, like those of the Lord, ought always to be throwing light on the path of the people in darkness. It ought to be possible, through the light we spread around, for men and women to become aware of their craftiness, selfishness, and wickedness. They ought to be brought to the point of shame and self-rebuke. Through observing us they ought to be able to discern the path that they should follow, and become aware of the duties that they should perform. They should see the destiny to which they are moving. They should become aware, through us, of the devices and craftiness of Satan; of the pitfalls and snares that he has set. No matter where we go we should be consistently shining.

If the light we spread around is the means of making people joyful and on this account to welcome us, that is a good thing. But if, on the other hand, it makes people angry and on this account to hate us, that also is a good thing. Irrespective of the effect we ought always to be a light.

Take the case of a Christian who is surrounded by non-Christians. If he can neither influence them by his virtues (thus making them respect him) nor influence them by his holiness (thus making them stand in awe of him), then woe is that Christian! For this only goes to show that he is not letting his light shine before men.

There are indeed a few Christians in the world who are engaged in spreading the light, but unfortunately their efforts are limited to words. They can preach quite acceptably; they can describe the beauties of the Lord; and they can indicate the path that men should follow. But before long their own shadow obscures this good teaching. For there is a considerable difference between what they say and what they do. It is like 'pointing the shafts towards the south and trying to move the cart to the north'. How sad! With their lips they preach holiness and righteousness but with their deeds they proclaim wickedness and uncleanness. What they preach is integrity but what they themselves practise is crookedness. What they preach is compassion but what they practise is marked by selfishness. A Christian like this not only fails to shine for the Lord, he is actually obscuring the Lord's glory. Not only is he unable to bring people to the Lord, he actually becomes a stumbling block. 'Woe to the world because of offences! For offences must come, but woe to that man by whom the offence comes!' (Matthew 18: 7).

Our first concern as Christians is not to perform some remarkable work for the Lord and to achieve something outstanding. Our first concern is to manifest the Lord in our lives, to conduct ourselves so that whenever people watch us they will see how they should live. When an artist paints a picture or does a carving, he places an actual object in front of him, and with this before him he paints his picture or does his carving. We call that object a model. Every Christian ought to be a model, a pattern. Thus if people are ignorant as to how they should order their life, all they need to do is to watch a Christian and then they should know. But the fundamental question is this, how many Christians today are in a position to serve as patterns for others? How many are worthy to be patterns?

Think for a moment of the body of Christians in the world. We will not include those who are totally void of spiritual life or those who are so cold that we can only regard them as frozen. Confining our thought to

Christians who are truly zealous we acknowledge that there are many of them who place their emphasis on labouring for the Lord, many of them who emphasise spiritual gifts, and many who emphasise knowledge. In contrast to this we find that those who emphasise holy living as a way of shedding the light are pitifully few. Of course I am not saying that it is wrong to emphasise work or gifts or knowledge. These things all have their value and their function. What I draw attention to is that if we only emphasise things like that while at the same time we neglect the duty of making our light shine through holy living, then we can by no means please God and by no means bring Him glory.

The fact is, when our Lord said, 'You are the light of the world', He had not finished His exhortation. He went on to say, 'Let your light so shine before men that they may see your good works and glorify your Father who is in heaven' (Matthew 5: 16). How true! It clearly shows that the process of glorifying God does not depend on our labours or our gifts or our knowledge; nor does it depend on what we preach. It depends on our 'good works'. In other words, on letting our light shine before men.

Now Christ is no longer living, as He once did, in this world. In that sense He is hidden from men's eyes. But we are His representatives and His ambassadors and it is through us that the world should now be able to see Him. We ought, through the way we live, to be revealing the same things to the world that Jesus revealed when He was on earth. As then, so now. Those who love Christ and His truth, when they see us spreading the light, may love and respect us also. At the same time those who hate the light and righteousness may end up by hating and attacking us also.

If in our own day we can make our light shine for the Lord in the way that He expects us to do, there is no question that in the future we shall 'shine forth as the sun in the kingdom of our Father' (Matthew 5: 43). Furthermore, 'they that be wise shall shine as the brightness of the firmament; and they that turn many to righteousness as the stars for ever and ever' (Daniel 12: 3).

11.
Temptation after success...

Matthew 14:10–23
John 6:10–15

Both of these passages record the same event. It was the miracle which took place in Galilee when Jesus took five loaves and two fishes and distributed them so that five thousand men were able to eat and be satisfied. But you will notice at then end of these passages that Matthew and John each record an event that is not recorded by the other. John tells us that after the Lord Jesus had divided the loaves the crowd sought to take him by force and to make Him king. He then retired to the mountain to be alone (John 6:15). What Matthew records, however, is that Jesus 'went up on a mountain by Himself to pray' (Matthew

14:23). This is not a case of the respective records of two people being in conflict, but a case of two people each recording one distinctive feature of the same event. John tells us why the Lord Jesus retired alone to the mountain while Matthew tells us what He did when He retired. Putting the two records together we find that because the crowd wanted to take Jesus by force to make Him king He then retired to the mountain, and when He arrived there what He did was to pray.

Reading these two passages we realise that after the Lord Jesus had performed the amazing miracle He was very severely tempted. When the crowd of several thousand people observed that with a minimal quantity of food He enabled so many people to eat and be satisfied, they concluded that if only they could make Him king of the Jews He would bestow upon them very great power. In next to no time the Jews would be well clothed and well fed. Further, with His power and authority, He would deliver the Jewish people from the oppression of Rome and He would recover for them the freedom that they had lost so long before. This was their hope, which they always kept alive in their hearts, and because of it they bent every effort to make Him king.

We can also call to mind another occurrence with similar features. After the Lord Jesus had been baptised He was led by the Spirit into the wilderness where He fasted for forty days. After that He was tempted by Satan. In one temptation the Devil showed Him all the nations of the world and said to Him, 'All this authority I will give you, and their glory; for that has been delivered to me, and I give it to whomever I wish. Therefore, if you will worship before me, all will be yours' (Luke 4:6,7). The Lord Jesus overcame Satan on that occasion by using a passage of Scripture.

On this later occasion, when He had used five loaves and two fishes to feed five thousand people, He was tempted in the same way. Furthermore, the

Five loaves and two fishes to feed five thousand people

temptation on this occasion was much fiercer than on the previous occasion. For what lay in front of Him now was the opportunity to become king of the Jews and to obtain glory and authority. He only needed to nod, so to speak, and the Jews would immediately swarm around him crying out 'Hail, the King!' In view of the miracle that He had just performed He was well aware that He could achieve something great for them. Within a short time He would lead them to victory over Rome and set up an independent kingdom. He would then undoubtedly receive the worship and respect not only of all the Jews but of the whole world also. In that way glory and all authority would be His.

When the Jews tried to take Him by force and to make Him king He would certainly feel that the temptation on this occasion was particularly severe, and that if he relaxed even for a moment He could easily be defeated by Satan. He knew that He needed strength from God and that He must call for the help and protection of God. He therefore retired alone to the mountain to pray. As a result of this prayer He was able to overcome the tempter. That night He walked on the water to join His disciples in the boat and to travel with them to the other side. Thus He overcame the temptation of Satan and, at the same time, He threw off the pressure of the people.

Are not our experiences similar to those of the Lord Jesus? Satan continually uses the glories and wealth and honours and the pleasures and comforts of the world to beguile us. He wants us to rebel against God and to become subject to himself. When Satan had no opportunity to use these things as temptations, he creates in our hearts countless imaginations, so that we may hanker after them. To bring all these temptations into subjection is by no means easy. It requires fervent prayer and it means that we must use the Word of God to resist him.

Yet more difficult than all this is the occasion when we have brought a particular work to completion and when because of it many people hold us in high esteem. Added to this are the opportunities it brings for us to become rich and famous. At such a time as this if we veer away from God even slightly it soon follows that we render our allegiance to Satan. It may well be that, when we first achieve success, we have not the slightest intention to use it for fame or profit or enjoyment. Maybe it is solely on account of our love for God and man that we do as we do. Yet after we have become successful we find that other people hold us in high esteem, and because they respect us – or may be in order to make use of us – they place before us the possibility of gaining many advantages. Satan meanwhile uses all these people and all this glory and gain to beguile us, with the object of making us submit to him and to turn our backs on God. So if we are not alert at times like this, and if we are not active in prayer, we shall undoubtedly fall into the snare of Satan.

Judging from the way in which many of the saints have experienced failure, we know that the time when believers achieve some success is just the time when they encounter the greatest temptations and the time when they face the gravest dangers. Many fine Christians fall and stumble at such a time as this, and many of them reach the point where they are unable to rise again.

Even during periods of poverty and distress we find Christians who continue to serve God zealously. Yet if the day comes when they become wealthy they depart from God completely and they go and worship Mammon. There are those who remain humble and spiritually minded Christians even when strangers to fame on the one hand and to notoriety on the other. But should the day come when they become famous they soon change their attitude and they become proud and profligate; through falling into sin they bring upon themselves much misfortune.

We need not speak simply of success in a secular business as a time when believers encounter this kind of temptation and danger, for even those who are engaged in work for God and who are used by Him to achieve great success – even they are liable to the same temptations and danger. Such a sequence of events is very familiar. We see workers who zealously serve God and before they achieve any success they are perfectly sincere and devout, and absolutely faithful. They are truly willing to leave everything in order to follow the Lord; they are full of love for their fellow-men; sin is an abhorrence to them. Since they are faithful to God in this way, God is using them. But after being used by God to do some great work the unexpected happens. They are honoured by men and become proud, and because they have the opportunity to become rich they go and serve Mammon. The love they had for God is changed into love for the world; the concern they had for others is changed into love for themselves; frugality is changed into greed; humility is changed into haughtiness; devoutness is changed into laxity; integrity is changed into deceit. Externally, maybe, they can still talk and preach as before, and they can still act energetically. But in their hearts they are already woefully empty. In course of time they leave the rails and they then end up in disgrace. I have known only too many like this. What a grievous thing this is!

We realise then that when Christians are in the position of having achieved some success they will certainly encounter this kind of temptation and danger. That being so, is there any way by which we can escape such dangers? The way of escape is to follow the pattern of the Lord Jesus. After completing a particular work successfully we must go quickly to the mountain and pray alone. Although it is not feasible for us to live permanently in the vicinity of the mountains, we certainly ought to seek a quiet place where we can have fellowship alone with God. We must cry to God to keep us so that we do not fall into the snares of Satan, so that even when people hold us in high esteem and applaud us we do not become proud; so that even when wealth is held out in front of us we do not become covetous; so that even though our possessions increase we do not develop a love of the world; and so that even though we become affluent we do not indulge ourselves and become dissolute and wasteful. For as soon as we experience success of some kind we can be sure that Satan will use both means and men to attack us from all directions and to hem us in. He will do all he can to blind our eyes.

We need to retire to a quiet place to meet God face to face, for only in that way will our hearts be at rest; we need to listen to His voice and to receive power from on high. Unless we do that we shall all unconsciously allow Satan to encircle us. While we think we are secure we are actually in a place of danger.

Satan's devices are comprehensive and thoroughgoing. He is able to attack us fiercely. It is only as we put our trust in the power of God that we can do battle with Satan. And it is when we have enjoyed success that Satan's attack is fiercest. All the more is it necessary for us to go alone into the presence of God.

It should be added, moreover, that after we have achieved some success we ought to go to God immediately. For if we delay even a little we shall allow Satan to get in first. The consequences then will be such as we dare not contemplate.

12.
Listening to one side only...

2 Samuel 16: 1–4
2 Samuel 19: 24–30

At the time that David was compelled by Absalom to abandon his kingdom and to flee for his life, Ziba brought the donkeys loaded with bread and wine to help supply the needs of David and his followers. Such an action, like 'transporting coal in snow', cannot do other than call forth our respect. And if we go on to listen to what Ziba had to say about Mephibosheth we shall find ourselves resenting Mephibosheth for showing himself completely devoid of conscience. Thus David turned to Ziba with the words, 'All that belonged to Mephibosheth is now yours' (2 Samuel 16: 4). This arrangement would truly

Like transporting coal in snow

seem appropriate. Here was a man apparently devoid of conscience who had proved undeserving of blessing. So all his property was taken away and handed over to Ziba who had acted in the manner of one 'transporting coal in the snow'. Who wouldn't approve of such a procedure?

Who would have imagined, however, that not only did what Ziba stated fail to correspond with the facts, but that what he stated was the opposite of the facts. The basest character was not Mephibosheth, but Ziba. The most admirable character was not Ziba, but Mephibosheth. Ziba tricked Mephibosheth and led away the donkeys that Mephibosheth had already prepared, so Mephibosheth was unable to follow David. Then Ziba himself made his way to David taking supplies of foodstuff in order to please him. He took the opportunity to vilify Mephibosheth. David was compeltely deceived by him and fully accepted his defamation of Mephibosheth's character. It was because of this that David gave all Mephibosheth's property to Ziba.

And what of Mephibosheth? Because of his lameness and because Ziba had taken away his donkeys Mephibosheth was prevented from following David. Nevertheless he was anxious about David as a fugitive, and so grieved at what had happened, that David was never for a moment out of his mind. That is why he had neither taken care of his feet, nor had he trimmed his moustache, and nor had he washed his clothes since the day that David had left home, and that is how it continued until the day when the king safely returned (2 Samuel 19: 24). It was not until David's return, however, that Mephibosheth was seen in his true light – they then saw his gratitude, his integrity, and his greatness. He was not in the least concerned about his own gain or loss, about his own glory or shame, and about his own advantages and disadvantages. He was single-minded in considering the interests of his benefactor, David. Alas! how many evil characters there are in the world today who are cunning and self-seeking like Ziba, and how few are those like Mephibosheth who are grateful and appreciative!

In spite of this, when Ziba vilifed Mephibosheth his lies were accepted by David as a true report. That is why David became angry with Mephibosheth and handed over the latter's possessions to Ziba. We can understand how ashamed he felt eventually when the true facts came to light. Although Mephibosheth himself made light of the occurrence, David must have pondered how rash he had been and how ready to believe slander even to laying a false charge against one who had loved him. How could he be other than ashamed of himself and how could he do other than blame himself?

At the time when Absalom set the rebellion in motion, and when this tragedy occurred in the family, David was no longer a young man. He was in fact of mature age. During the decades preceeding these events he had suffered greatly at the hand of Saul, and after he became King he had for a number of years carried the major responsibility for the affairs of state. He was moreover a devout worshipper of God. When it came to spiritual understanding, and when it came to having experience of the world, David was certainly superior to all others. In spite of all this he was still not immune to listening only to one side of the issue. He was thus deceived into believing a slander, and he was consequently used by evil men to perpetrate an injustice on one who loved him.

If that is true of a man of superior qualifications and achievements like David, what if one of inferior attainemnts acted like him in listening only to one side? Truly we ought to be especially watchful, no matter who it is who speaks in our presence of the bad reputation and wrongdoing of other people. For you do not know, when it comes down to it, whether words uttered in this way are true or not, or whether they constitute slander or not. Why do people engage in vilifying others? The reasons are varied. Some do so in order to profit themselves at the expense of others. Others do it because they envy those who are better off than themselves. Yet others do it because of ill-will. Should you be brought into touch with people in these categories and they talk of other people in a derogatory way, will you unquestioningly believe what they say? If you do so you may not only help wicked men to gain advantages, you may also cause good men to suffer harm. The day will come when you discover the real facts and you will be filled with shame and embarrassment. There will be no place for you to hide.

There are many people who are not corrupt in the same way as the types referred to above, yet circumstances sometimes arise which cause them to clash with other people. They see only their side of the argument and fail to see the other side of the argument. They get the impression that those on the other side are ruthlessly seeking their own personal gain. If, in addition, they are sensitive, or if they are inclined to be suspicious, and if they regard their own appraisal of the situation as being indisputable fact, the situation becomes even more serious. Holding firmly to this poisition they become indignant and upset, and in order to give vent to their own spirit of unrest they use all the strength to propagate what they regard as the shortcomings of the other side. They forget that the other side also has its own argument and its own line of reasoning. It may be that this other side regards the first side in the same way – that is, as seeking their own personal gain. In all the conflicts that take place throughout the world, there is usually something to say on both sides.

When the opposing side is made up of people who are of a sympathetic nature, who are ready to forbear, and who are prepared to endure misunderstanding, the whole situation is far easier to manage. But where in all the world can you find people so magnanimous that they are prepared to consider the viewpoint of the other side? Alas! they are rare indeed.

When two parties are in opposition to each other, no matter which of the two you come into touch with, if you only listen to that one side you will certainly be liable to make a false judgement. But if you listen carefully to the reasons adduced by both sides, and you carefully investigate the causes of the estrangement, you will probably find that both sides have reasons and that both sides are without reasons. Since both sides have grounds for their position neither side is prepared to give way. Do you recall the words of the philosopher? 'To be willing in all things to consider others is the highest form of scholarship.' Alas! the possessors of scholarship like this are as rare as phoenix feathers and as the horns of unicorns, so whenever conflict occurs between person and person the trouble piles up layer upon layer without end.

So whenever we come across someone who talks of the evil doings of other people we must be extremely watchful, never lightly accepting the arguments of one side only lest we form a wrong impression of those on the other side. Whenever we want to help settle disputes and to clear up misunderstandings, or whenever we have responsibility to enquire into the real facts in a confused situation, we must investigate the reasoning on both sides and pay close attention to the arguments put forward on both sides, as well as to the inadmissable arguments advanced by either side. In that way we should be able to discover where the difficulty lies and where the misunderstanding has arisen. By listening only to one side we shall not only fail to make a useful contribution but we shall add fuel to the flames. And we ourselves may well be caught up into the vortex.

If we are unduly sympathetic to one particular side and unjustifiably support it, those on that side will stubbornly stick to the view that they are in the right and that the other side is in the wrong. On the other hand, the other side will take note that our judgement is unfair and they will then transfer their anger to us. The confusion will no longer be confined to two sides; it will now be extended to three sides. In that case it would have been far better for us not to have given any help at all than to have given the help that we did.

Those who are temperamentally hasty and find it difficult to come to impartial decisions must be particularly watchful of themselves. Experience has taught us that the real facts in situations like this rarely correspond with appearances. Even a slight lack of caution may lead to catastrophe. The fact that when David listened to the one-sided statements of Ziba the consequences were less serious than they might have been was due entirely to the fact that the one to suffer from it was the great-hearted and high-minded Mephibosheth. But men of that calibre do not number more than one in thousands. But suppose the vilification of wicked men like Ziba is aimed at someone who is not high-minded like Mephibosheth, what would be the consequences then?

13.
Understanding and doing the will of God...

Romans 12: 1,2

'I beseech you therefore, brethren, by the mercies of God, that you present your bodies a living sacrifice, holy, acceptable to God, which is your reasonable service.

'And do not be conformed to this world, but be transformed by the renewing of your mind, that you may prove what is that good and acceptable and perfect will of God.'

Ephesians 5: 17
'Therefore do not be unwise, but understanding what the will of the Lord is.'

'The Will of God' is an expression that is constantly on the lips of many earnest Christians. For they desire with all their hearts to understand God's Will. Yet at the same time they often treat the concept erroneously. Some Christians regard that which is expressed by certain people whom they look up to as the will of God. Even when these things are obviously not the will of God they persist in thinking in their hearts that they are. In the course of time they meet misfortune and only then do they regretfully discover that it was due to their own misconceptions. Other Christians are not aroused to the truth for the whole of their lives, and from first to last they regard either their own ideas or else the ideas put to them by other people as being the will of God. Such people are much to be pitied

But what are the facts? When you come down to it, is it difficult or is it not difficult to understand God's will? We may answer that it is both difficult to understand and also easy to understand. Even Christians who are mature and experienced and spiritually minded sometimes have difficulty in knowing the mind of God. On the other hand we may say that God's will is easy to understand in that it has been revealed in the Bible. If only we will search the Scriptures diligently and plant God's teaching in all its abundance in our hearts, it will then be easy to understand God's will. It is true that God has not written in detail how we ought to do certain things, nor has He written in detail how we should avoid other things. But He has revealed to us the principles which we ought to follow. He shows us how we ought to serve God and glorify God. He shows us how we should honour our parents, and how we should bring up children. He shows us how husband and wife should live together; He shows us how master and servant should treat each other. He shows us how we should treat our neighbours, and He shows us how we should treat our enemies. He shows us how we should handle our affairs. He shows us how we should act as human beings. He shows us how we should acquire money. He shows us how we should use money. He shows us how we should work and He shows us how we should rest. He shows us how we should take precautions against temptation and He shows us how to resist Satan. He shows us the danger of covetousness and He shows us the harm of unrestrained indulgence. He shows us how we should preach the Gospel. He shows us how we should guard against ourselves. So long as we plant these principles firmly in our hearts, then no matter what we encounter, God's Spirit can use these principles to instruct us and to guide us. In that way we need not veer either to the right hand or to the left hand, and we can walk always within the will of God.

Since the will of God is as easy to understand as this, why is it that the majority of Christians continue to walk as if in a dense fog? If it is not a case of their not clearly understanding it, then it is a case of their regarding either their own ideas or the ideas of other people as the will of God. We can get an answer to our question from the Scriptures referred to above. 'Do not be conformed to this world, but be transformed by the renewing of your mind!' Only thus can we come to an understanding of 'that good and acceptable and perfect will of God'. In other words, if we continue as before to be conformed to the world in which we live, if our attitudes are no different from what they were before we turned to the Lord, and if we still hanker after the world – its wealth, its fame, its vainglory, its enjoyments, and its amusements – then we are not in a position to find out what is the good and acceptable and perfect will of God. If we cannot understand God's will, it is not because God's will is obscure and difficult to understand. It is rather because our eyes have been veiled by the things of the world we live in. When a believer refuses to get rid of the wordly things that veil his eyes, and he is not transformed by the renewing of his mind, then no matter how long he has believed in the Lord, no matter how familiar he is with the Bible, and no matter how zeolous he is, he will still fail to understand God's will.

There are some Christians who know God's will and yet they do not treat it as God's will; they put their own will in its place. The reason is that they still aim to enjoy the good things offered by the world and to fulfil their worldly aspirations. Let us take an example. Suppose a Christian has just left college and he is seeking employment. He receives two offers at the same time. By accepting the first he would enjoy a substantial income, but it would mean sacrificing his integrity – telling untruths, deceiving, and acting in an underhand way. If he accepts the second offer, however, the work would be law-abiding, honest, and of benefit to society. Yet although the salary would be adequate, it would be lower than he would get in the first position, and he would have little to put into savings. According to the teaching of the Bible there is not the slightest doubt that it would be God's will for him to accept the latter. But supposing he really coveted the pleasures and wealth of the world, what explanation would he give for his choice? How would he justify his choice? He could say, 'By accepting the first offer I shall have more money with which to help the church and with which to promote the work of God. Moreover I could bring relief to poverty-stricken believers and do things to benefit many people'. In that way he could argue that the first of the two offers is the one that represents the will of God.

Take another example. Suppose a young Christian woman is approached by two young men with a view to marriage. The first is not a believer, but he comes from an affluent family, and his qualifications are very high. The second is a Christian but, with no capital and nothing saved up, he is barely in a position to provide a family with food and warmth. His education moreover is inferior to that of the first. The teaching of the Bible is that we should not be unequally yoked together with unbelievers, and in the light of that there should be no doubt whatever as to which of the two offers (if either) she should accept – obviously the second. But if she aspires to wordly advantages and pleasures, and opts for the first, she could still argue to herself that it was God's will. She could say, 'By marrying the one who does not believe I shall be able to help him and lead him to the Lord. The one who is already a believer does not need outside guidance in the same way. It is for the Lord's sake that I am willing to marry the one who is not a believer in the hope that I can save him. This therefore is certainly the will of God'.

Let us cite another example. Suppose a young man wishes to take the entrance examination to a certain college but his age, alas! is several years beyond the age-limit. Someone makes the suggestion, therefore, that he should tell a lie and register his age as below the age limit. According to the teaching of the Bible there is not the slightest doubt that this is not God's will. But because of his hope to graduate, and thus to obtain a qualification that is demanded by the world (so that in the future he can the more easily find a post in society), he decides to engage in deceit. But he justifies himself as follows: 'My hope is to obtain greater knowledge and skill so that in the future I can better serve God and better serve people. Although I wrongly registered my age as being a little less than it really is, yet I first prayed over it and asked God that, if it was not His will, he would cause me to fail in my entrance examination. In the event I passed my examination successfully and it is thus a testimony to me that the path I have chosen is the will of God.'

According to the teaching of the Bible the three choices I have postulated above cannot be in accordance with God's will. What happened was that the eyes of the people concerned were veiled – or blinded – by their love for the things of the world. They could no longer see clearly. They are still conformed to this world, their minds have not been renewed, and they have not been transformed. They have not fulfilled the conditions and as a consequence they cannot understand what is the good and acceptable and perfect will of God. To put this reasoning positively, if we are desirous of knowing the good and acceptable and perfect will of God, we must ask God to change our hearts, which are still conformed to the world, and to renew our minds so that our thoughts and attitudes are transformed. Once we become one with Him, which means that we love what he loves and hate what He hates, it will become easy for us to know what is God's will.

Another question arises. Do we or do we not obey and follow the truths that we already know? The answer to this question has a good deal to do with our understanding God's will. There are features in the will of God that are extremely easy to understand. These were as clear to us after we believed in the Lord as pointing to the palm of our hand. If we can strive assiduously to carry out what we have learned, the

Holy Spirit will then take us a step further and He will teach us to understand more difficult things. But if we fail to follow that which we already know, not only shall we be unable to press ahead and to understand the things that are more difficult, we shall find that the kind of truths that we originally understood now elude us. 'To everyone who has, more will be given, and he will have abundance; but from him who does not have will be taken away even what he has' (Matthew 25: 29).

If a believer does no more than keep on saying that he wants to understand the will of God, and if he is unwilling to make the necessary efforts to put into practice what he already knows, he will never understand God's will so long as he lives. It is an observable fact that the lives of many Christians are still marked by all kinds of unrighteous characteristics. They are self-seeking, they tell untruths and act deceitfully, they covet riches and fame, they are prone to envy and malice. They are aware that all these things are repugnant to God, but they are unwilling to get rid of them. They know what is pleasing to God – being filial children, loving their brethren, having compassion on the poor, being merciful to enemies, acting honestly in business, being chaste in all relations with members of the opposite sex, and not being covetous of other people's property. Christians understand these standards as clearly as they know that two and two are four. But what they do in practice does not harmonise with what they know and understand in theory. Yet they never stop saying that they are seeking to know the will of God. Such a reputation makes one very concerned (lit. to have headache and heartache).

Another point has already been touched on. Our familiarity with the Scriptures has a strong bearing on

Unless he observes the flowers closely he will obviously get no impression of them

our understanding of God's will. Since much of God's will is revealed to us in the Bible, naturally the more familiar we are with the Bible the more we shall understand God's will. But this requires us to spend time in diligent study of the Scriptures; it requires us to turn the passages over and over in our mind as well as memorising important verses. There are no rewards for the lazy. If you want to have a fuller understanding of how a particular person thinks you must listen carefully to his words. You must pay close attention to what he says and you must turn this over in your mind. It is the same if you want to understand the mind of God. When you search the Scriptures you must on no account adopt the attitude of a man who rides a horse while looking at the wayside flowers, being satisfied to glance at them briefly in passing. Unless he observes the flowers closely he will obviously get no deep impression of them. Further, you must not study the Bible in the same way that you study history, geography, and biology. Theological students are prone to study the Bible in this way. When we read the Bible we ought to adopt the attitude of a son who is reading a letter from his father who is away from home. The son will be concerned with his father's instructions for him – how to be a filial son, how to love his brothers and sisters, how to take his place in the world, how to be diligent, how to manage a family, and how to beware of the blandishments of evil men. The son gives attention to these things so that his father who is away may feel contented and happy, for the son will do his duty to the best of his ability. As a result of reading this letter the son will be more conscious of his father's love and he will know what advantages the father is conferring on him for his enjoyment and happiness. Only if we adopt an attitude like this when we read the Bible can we have grounds for hoping that through our reading we can understand more of God's will, and only thus can we get the greatest profit possible for our exercise. But those who read the Bible simply as a text-book will never obtain such benefits.

The question arises, to what extent do we need to make a practice of asking God to show us His will? There are certain believers who follow the practice, before they engage in any activity whatever, of asking God whether it is His will or not. Even regarding those things that are patently according to His will these Christians find it necessary to enquire of God before they embark on them. Now if such Christians are sincere and straightforward in making this enquiry no more is involved than spending a little extra time. But there are times when Christians ask for guidance about a matter that is clearly the will of God and instead of following it they choose to regard it as not being God's will. So they do nothing about it. Rather than ask about God's will in circumstances like this is it not better to refrain from asking?

The only reason that we ask God to show us His will ought to be that we are not clear about it in our own minds. Certainly, when we are not clear, we ought to ask God for guidance. But not otherwise. Some years ago there was a preacher who said this: 'No matter what I do, I first enquire whether it is according to God's will or not. Even when I eat, I first enquire whether it is God's will that I eat.' Maybe there are those who regard such a preacher as being very sincere, but in my view this teaching is quite wrong. Personally I do not enquire, when I eat, whether or not it is God's will that I should do so. So long as God allows me to eat I give thanks for the food and then I eat. For I clearly know at the time it is God's intention that I should eat. Nor do I enquire of God every evening whether or not He permits me to sleep, because I clearly know that when I am tired God wants me to sleep. When anyone in my family is taken ill, if there is no urgent business awaiting my attention, I go and help look after him or her. When my neighbours encounter adversity and trouble, provided it is not bound up with anything doubtful I go to help them.

Apart from these there are many other things that I clearly know are not in accordance with God's will. I neither do them nor do I enquire of God about them. For example, someone may urge me to buy a lottery ticket, or to buy things that are of doubtful origin. I refuse them on the spot. Nor do I persist in asking God whether it is permissible for me to do these things, for I am perfectly clear in my mind that they are not according to God's will. Or maybe someone does something dishonest and then requests me to act as his guarantor. Again, I decline on the spot. I do not need to ask God whether He permits it, for I clearly know that God would on no account permit me to help people to engage in swindling. If you clearly know that a certain thing is according to God's will and yet you still go and ask Him about it, it will show that your attitude is equivocal. You are still hoping that God will permit you to do whatever it is so that you may secure certain benefits. But this is just the opportunity for Satan to lead you along the path or error and to lead you into sin.

It may also be said that the extent to which we understand God's will is in direct ratio to the extent of our fellowship with God. The more a son chats with his father and the nearer he keeps to him, the more he will understand his father's mind. Reasoning of this kind we can readily understand. It can be applied also to our fellowship with God. A Christian who spends much time in prayer and who often waits quietly in God's presence will naturally have a greater understanding of God's will than those who do not. God has many purposes – noble and profound and beautiful – which He will reveal only to those who spend time with Him.

To go back a step, if we do not maintain our fellowship with God, we reach the point where we are unable to understand even the truths that are commonplace. We may even reach the point where we turn truth and error upside down and mix up black and white. It is possible for a believer, in normal circumstances, to neglect his privilege of approaching God and having fellowship with Him. But suppose a day comes when he is faced with problems that are hard to solve or when his affairs become difficult to manage. In a situation like that he will want to understand God's will and to call on Him for help. But unless God has mercy on him in a special way he may fail to achieve his aim.

There are times in our lives when we come as it were to a fork in the road, and we do not know which of the two roads before us we should take; we do not know which is according to God's will. What should we do? Apart from our humbling ourselves before God and seeking His guidance, there may be a place for asking advice from others. It may be that we are in touch with devout believers who are more experienced than we are and who have practical knowledge of finding out God's will. We could approach them and ask their advice. The reason that God has given a variety of gifts to the church is so that believers as members of the body may help each other.

But do not enquire of those who lack piety, those who are too young and inexperienced, and those who invariably say what they think you want them to say. The advice of people like this will never help you to understand God's will; in fact it may lead you into sin and danger. When Rehoboam succeeded to the throne of Israel, all the people pleaded with him to lighten their load. He could not make up his mind whether to agree to this or not. So he approached the older men who had previously served his father and asked them to counsel him in the matter. The advice they gave was excellent. They counselled him to respect the feelings of the people and to agree to their request. Alas! Rehoboam in his ignorance refused to follow their advice. What he did was to turn to the young men who had been brought up with him and to ask advice from them. These young men had not the slightest love for the people and they sought nothing but their own advantages. Moreover they were entirely without experience, having a very limited outlook (like frogs at the bottom of a well), and were utterly ignorant of how to deal with difficulties along the road. Knowing that Rehoboam had first sought the counsel of the older men and then turned to themselves, they realised that he had no desire to follow the older men's advice. So they fell in line with what they perceived to be Rehoboam's wishes, urging him to reject the petition of the people and to answer them very harshly. As a result of all this they brought upon themselves great misfortune. The people revolted against Rehoboam and they set up Jeroboam as king in his place. The consequence was that Israel now became two kingdoms.

So rather than ask advice of those who are young and ignorant – and who would merely say what they think you want them to say – it is preferable not to ask the advice of anyone.

'Do not be conformed to this world, but be transformed by the renewing of your mind, that you may prove what is that good and acceptable and perfect will of God!'

14.
Those who deserve to be accursed...

Galatians 1: 6-10

'If anyone preaches any other gospel to you than what you have received, let him be accursed' (verse 9).

Astonishing indeed! How could Paul, a man full of love, make use of words so stern and terrible as this? Was it not the apostle Paul who once wrote to the Romans -- 'Bless them which persecute you: bless and curse not'? (12: 14) In the light of that, how could he himself resort to cursing? Was it not evidence of lack of love? Is it not a case of words and deeds failing to harmonize?

The fact is, we have no need to be astonished. All we need to do is to enquire carefully as to the reason Paul uttered these words. Once we have done that we shall be completely satisfied that these words do not in any way conflict with his admonition to 'bless and curse not'.

Certain people in the churches of Galatia were disseminating the teaching that the Gentiles, without being circumcised, could not be saved. Teaching of this nature was absolutely contrary to the gospel of God's grace, and people were being misdirected by it to tread the path of error. As a consequence of this they were putting their trust in the Law – the purpose of which was to bring a consciousness of sin – and they were failing to put their trust only in Christ and Him crucified.

What a precious thing is the gospel of God's salvation! How authentic! How sacred! How dynamic! Yet there are those today who dare to put forward their own ideas as a substitute. Their presumption is astounding! Their teaching is utterly harmful! Inevitably therefore, although God has no desire whatever to curse anyone, those who act in this way bring a curse upon themselves. We see therefore why God makes use of His servant Paul to stress the fact of such a curse. It is in order that those who listen to his words may realise what a serious matter it is to change the substance of the gospel – the gospel of God. For those who do so are in danger of incurring God's anger. At the same time the apostle's words are not spoken merely as a warning – they are spoken to encourage the whole church of God to maintain its faith unshaken in the one true gosepl. The words are also intended to strengthen the readers in their resolve not to be deceived by false gospels. In uttering these words the apostle Paul was not pronouncing a curse on anyone. As God's representative he was simply announcing the threatened curse in just the same way that he would proclaim the fact of the gospel.

What is the teaching of Romans 12: 14 – 'Bless them which persecute you; bless and curse not!'? Paul is here teaching believers that they must not recompense evil with evil; they must bless those who persecute them and they must always refrain from cursing them. This exhortation is necessary because when people of the world are insulted or ill-treated it is natural for them to retaliate. If they are unable to offer resistance physically they resort to cursing with their lips. In that way they manifest their hatred.

But God knows the weakness of His children. When they are insulted or ill-treated, and when they are unable to offer physical resistance, they too find it difficult to avoid giving vent to curses. That is why God has charged them through his servant to 'bless and curse not'.

It is clear then that we ought to refrain from cursing those who wrong us and harm us. We ought to react in the same way that our Lord did. It is written of him that 'when He was reviled (he) reviled not again; when he suffered he threatened not' (1 Peter 2: 23). We ought to pray for those who harm us as our Lord did. Jesus prayed, 'Father, forgive them; for they know not what they do' (Luke 23: 34). On no account must we hate those who hate us; on no account must we curse those who persecute us. But if God constrains us to announce His own curse on those who rebel against Him, we cannot remain silent. When the Lord Jesus was attacked and persecuted by evil men, He never opened His mouth. Yet when God wanted Him to pronounce a curse on the hypocritical scribes and Pharissees He did not hesitate to cry with a loud voice: 'Woe unto you, scribes and Pharisees, hypocrites!' (Matthew 23: 13ff). Note also how He addressed those who refused to repent. 'I tell you, no; but unless you repent, you will all likewise perish'

(Luke 13: 3,5).

How shall we describe this word which was used by the Lord? Was it a curse or was it not? Does it have the same connotation as when we ourselves are roused to curse people as a result of anger? No! Certainly not! Never at any time did the Lord resort to cursing in order to give vent to anger. Indeed at no time did He allow anger to arise in His heart. What He was doing, in using these words, was to announce a curse on behalf of God. And even in announcing the curse He still desired that those concerned would repent and flee from the curse. For it is clear that if they come to repentance the curse will be rescinded. But if they totally harden their hearts the curse will pursue its course, and there will be no way whatever to escape from it.

Now it is clearly demonstrated in the Bible that although God through one of His servants may pronounce a curse on certain people, yet until that curse actually takes effect it is still not too late for those who are under the curse to reform themselves (lit. to rein in the horses on the edge of the precipice). It is still possible for them to awaken to a sense of having transgressed, and if they do that then God Himself is prepared to rescind the threatened calamity. The example I have in mind of course is that which is recorded for use in the Book of Jonah (3: 4–10). The people of Ninevah had sinned before God and He not only decided to destroy them but He also fixed the day on which this judgement would come to pass. Since even the day had been fixed, how could anything be altered? Any change of mind on God's part seemed impossible. Yet God still desired that the people would repent, and He still provided an opportunity for the people to do so. That is why He sent the prophet Jonah into the city to announce its impending doom. For although God's curse lay upon it, yet the people still had the chance to 'rein in the horses at the edge of the precipice'. As soon as they heard the warning they confessed their sins before God, and thus escaped the implementation of the curse that God had already pronounced on it. We see, in the light of this, that even though a seemingly irrevocable curse is pronounced, so long as it has not actually come to pass it is still possible for those who are cursed to escape. How vast is God's love! How great His forbearance!

Let us turn back to Galatians and give further thought to the people who are there described as deserving to be cursed. 'Though we or an angel from heaven, preach any other gospel unto you than that which we have preached unto you, let him be accursed' (verse 8). Even should it be angels – and not mere human beings – who preach another gospel, they still deserve to be accursed. What a solemn thing this is! And can we blame God for being too severe? Certainly not. The gospel is a great and wonderful way of salvation that God in His infinite wisdom and power and compassion has provided for mankind. Wordly institutions may change, but not the gospel. Not even by a hairsbreadth may we change it. When anyone preaches another gospel, and by so doing distorts the gospel of Christ, he is not only inflicting harm on men he is also insulting God. It is blasphemy.

During the lifetime of the apostle Paul the gospel was already being preached in many areas, but it was only in the churches of Galatia that anyone was preaching another gospel. To Paul this was a source of great grief and anxiety, and he wrote this letter to the churches of Galatia in order to counter this erroneous preaching of another gospel. He warned the believers against departing from the rightful path, and in the name of God he announced this fearful curse.

Coming down to modern times we find that in the 19th century there also arose another gospel. It was a different gospel that quickly spread to many churches. In fact those who preached this other gospel announced the fact unashamedly. They called it the 'social gospel'. It was not a case of propagating a different religion. It was not a case of using a different Bible. They still professed to believe in Christ and to preach Christ. They used the same Bible. Moreover, the Bible that they held in their hands did not delete the letter to the Galatians. But in spite of that they nevertheless preached a different gospel, and they did not hesitate to acknowledge that it was a different gospel. Now we know for a certainty that if they refuse to accept God's warning, and if they persist in refusing to repent, the curse will inevitably descend upon them. It may be that they themselves have no fears on this score, but I am myself very fearful on their account.

And what of those who preach this other gospel? How do they explain themselves? What they say amounts to this: 'To preach that Jesus atoned for men's sin, and to urge people to repent and believe in Jesus in order to inherit eternal life, is a system that caters only for the individual. In fact we may call it a gospel for the individual. Such a gospel is very narrow in its scope and benefits only oneself. What we want to do now is to preach a broad gospel that brings benefit to others. It is not our practice to exhort people to believe in Jesus in order that they may inherit eternal life; what we do is to exhort people to embrace the high ideals of Jesus and to pattern themselves on his sublime character. In dependence on the measureless love of Jesus we are in a position to transform society and to eliminate all war, and murder, and violence, and robbery, and pain and disease. Society as a whole can thus be saved and the world will then become the kingdom of heaven. Is not such a gospel infinitely superior to a gospel that is concerned only with the happiness or misery and the life or death of individuals?'

When we hear such an argument for the first time it sounds very plausible. Not to be concerned about the happiness or misery of individuals, or about the salvation of individuals, and to be concerned rather about the wellbeing of society as a whole – and all this appears on the surface to harmonize with what Jesus taught about self-denial. But when we pause for a moment, and carefully analyse talk of this kind, we find that the speakers have not really put their trust in Jesus yet they call themselves Christians and preachers of the gospel. Since basically they have never put their trust in Jesus they are incapable of preaching the gospel of Jesus. That is why they use the expression 'social gospel' to dignify what they preach.

I repeat, they do not accept the gospel of Jesus according to which He shed His blood to atone for sin, nor do they believe the promise that those who repent and believe inherit eternal life. They regard those who have such beliefs as ignorant and superstitious. However, it would not do for them to state clearly that they do not accept such doctrines, for in that case they could no longer describe themselves as Christians. They have therefore come up with the notion that the salvation of individuals is to be regarded as something selfish. In that way they not only cover their own lack of belief, they also condemn true Christians for what they choose to regard as the latter's shortcoming. They give the appearance of acting more lovingly than true Christians, whereas they are guilty of misleading people. Let me explain what I mean.

Obviously we cannot do other than recognise the need to eliminate killing and violence and robberies and diseases and pain – all of which characterise life in society today. But we ought also to understand that all these calamities are ultimately and totally the results of sin. So long as you do not solve the question of sin you cannot even begin to talk about anything else. Yet the problem of sin can never be solved by the intelligence of man. But thanks be to God! He sent His Son into the world expressly to solve this problem! Christ shed His blood and gave His life for our sins. When we repent and believe in Him all our sins are forgiven. At the same time He imparts His life to us and we are transformed from within. Love of sinning gives way to love of holiness and virtue; the heart that faced towards darkness now becomes a heart that faces righteousness and life; the love of self gives place to love for others. The inner transformation is accompanied by a transformation of the whole life. This is exactly what the Bible tells us: 'If anyone is in Christ, he is a new creation; old things have passed away; behold, all things have become new' (2 Cor. 5: 17).

More than this. The Christ who died on the cross also rose from the dead. He has overcome the power of death. 'Inasmuch then as the children have partaken of flesh and blood, He also Himself likewise shared in the same, that through death He might destroy him who had the power of death, that is, the devil' (Hebrews 2: 14). To Him also was given authority both in heaven and on earth (Matthew 28: 18). His resurrection gave evidence not only of the completion of the work of redemption but also of His power to save all who put their trust in Him. This means deliverance not only from the punishment of sin but also from the power of sin. When a person repents and believes in Christ the problem of his sin is solved at the root. This is how sin is dealt with in society. If a person does not put his trust in Christ he cannot save even himself, how can he speak of changing society?

When we urge people to repent and to believe in the Lord, in order that they may receive eternal life, we are charged by preachers of the social gospel of selfishly seeking individual gain. If they are reported correctly, I would like to ask them a question. If they are seeking to reduce the suffering of mankind, by preaching the social gospel, are they not also selfishly seeking gain? How can they say that when you seek people's happiness for a few decades you are showing your love for them but when you seek their happiness for eternity you are seeking personal gain? I wonder if those who talk in this way are conscious of their mental gymnastics. If it is wrong for us to exhort people to repent and to believe in the Lord, in order that they may obtain eternal life, then by the same reasoning it is wrong for us to do anything to avoid their freezing or starving to death. On the other hand, if it is right for an individual to seek survival by scheming to obtain food and clothing, then it is also right to seek eternal life. In fact more so. It is also entirely reasonable that one who has been saved should seek to lead others along the same path of salvation.

Those who preach the social gospel assert that they want to use their gospel to change society. We are very willing to be shown the societies that they have transformed. We are even more willing to be shown whether or not they themselves have been transformed. 'Every good tree bears good fruit, but

Every good tree bears good fruit

a bad tree bears bad fruit. A good tree cannot bear bad fruit, nor can a bad tree bear good fruit' (Matthew 7: 17,18). We should look closely at the lives of those who preach the social gospel. for if a man has no compunction about deceiving people in matters of the Faith, how can we expect him to be living a life of virtue? If a man has no fear even of a curse pronounced by God, what limits can there be to the brazen hardening of his heart? Yet they still talk about changing society. If that is'nt talking in one's sleep, what is it?

Once again I ask the question, 'What is the greatest need of mankind?' Is it extravagant clothes? Is it lavish food? Is it a congenial occupation? Is it tranquility? Is it a higher education? Is it adequate medical provision? Is it upright politics? Is it a comprehensive system of law? Is it a higher level of society? Is it harmony among the nations? Is it the reform of our habits? Is it the establishment of virtue? All these are the needs of mankind. But the greatest need of all is not among them. Mankind's greatest need is to come to God for forvgiveness of sin in order to obtain eternal life. Whether people acknowledge it or not, their greatest need is to be brought into touch with God. For God is the source of all happiness. But they have been cut off from God by sin and they themselves are unable to bridge the gap. What else can people do but endure pain and await the onset of death?

But thanks be to God! He has prepared a wonderful way of salvation for needy mankind. The Lord Jesus Christ has laid down His life on the cross and accomplished the work of redemption. The sins of all who believe are forgiven. They are justified before God and become His children. The life they inherit is incorruptible. This is the gospel to meet men's fundamental need. Other than this there is no gospel. Other than this there is no doctrine that can truthfully be described as 'gospel'. To compare the so-called social gospel with this gospel is like comparing a gilded coin made of lead to a coin made of gold. Put them side by side – the true and the false, the good and the bad – and you can easily distinguish between them. Facts can swallow up argument.

Through the preaching of the saving grace of God countless numbers have been saved. They have turned to God in repentance and faith and their lives have been wonderfully transformed. Even the hard-hearted and the loveless have confessed their sins before God. Those who once regarded themselves as righteous have humbled themselves before God and have bowed before Him in contrition. People who were once fierce and violent have become like sheep. People who once sought their own interests now seek the interests of others. People who were once discouraged are now aflame with zeal. Those who were once broken-hearted and those who once wept are now greatly comforted.

The protagonists of the social gospel criticise these people and condemn their activities as emotional, and they charge these people with being superstitious and deceived. The fact is, not only does the preaching of the social gospel fail to get better results than this, they even fail to match up to them.

There is another point to comment on. While the gospel of the saving grace of God has the power to transform people, the preachers of this gospel almost invariably enounter opposition and attack from many quarters. Unbelievers charge them with being superstitious; evil-doers say they revile people. Yet the preachers of the social gospel are free from attacks of this nature. Unbelievers never deride them; evil-doers do not hate them. In fact unbelievers will convene welcome meetings for them and co-operate with them in the task of re-structuring society. These features only demonstrate further that the social gospel derives from men and not from God. The words of John confirm this: 'They are of the world. Therefore they speak as of the world, and the world hears them' (1 John 4: 5). Only the gospel of the saving grace of God is the power of God to save all that we believe. 'I am not ashamed of the gospel of Christ', wrote Paul, 'for it is the power of God to salvation for everyone who believes' (Romans 1: 16).

This gospel is the gospel that saves, It is also the gospel that destroys the work of the devil. Naturally the devil will mobilise all the power he can to attack those who proclaim the gospel. Since the social gospel does not save people it poses no threat to the work of Satan. So why should Satan interfere with it? In fact the social gospel can even be used to aid him. For it can mislead and confuse people. Why should the devil oppose it?

Maybe there are people who would defend the social gospel by arguing as follows. 'Although the social gospel doesn't save people, and it cannot be a substitute for the gospel of the saving grace of God, yet by its very nature it can help people morally and it can promote the progress of society. Is it not enough that we ourselves desist from preaching it? Why should we go out of our way to oppose it?'

In order to answer this question I will offer an illustration. Suppose an infectious disease breaks out, in a certain city, and begins to spread. If those infected are not speedily cured not one of them has a hope of saving his life. But a doctor is within reach who has discovered an effective drug for the treatment of this particular disease. As a result the lives of many people have been saved. Now suppose in that city there is also a quack medicine seller. He has observed that the sale of a drug to cure that particular disease can make one rich. So he manufactures and markets a bogus medicine, and asserts that it can cure the disease in question. But in fact it is a fake and has no efficacy whatever. Now his medicine contains no poison; the drawback is only that its ingredients are ineffective for the purpose claimed. The danger does not lie in the drug being poisonous or harmful. The danger is that the people who are infected with the disease will take the fake medicine and then relax; they now see no need whatever to buy the genuine article. And it still results in their losing their lives. Now think for a moment! Is it not the seller of the fake medicine who is responsible for the loss of life?

No one is free from the disease of sin. It is a disease that, left to itself, will bring about spiritual death. The only medicine that will cure this disease is the gospel. The so-called 'social gospel' is a counterfeit medicine conjured up by the devil. We acknowledge that in this counterfeit medicine there is no poison. It is nevertheless true that those who put their faith in it now consider that they are safe. As a result they see no need to put their trust in the true gospel. That being so, how can you say that those who proclaim a counterfeit gospel are free from the guilt of causing spiritual death?

Here then is the reason that we must not only preach the genuine gospel but that we must exert all our strength to oppose the false gospel. It may be that some will argue against us as follows. 'The preachers of the social gospel neither oppose you nor attack you. So why do you attack them? Doesn't this show that they are wide in their sympathies whereas you are narrow?' In answering this question I revert to my illustration. At a time when genuine medicine and counterfeit medicine are being sold in the same city, who is it attacks whom? Is it the doctor who discovered the efficacious medicine who now attacks the seller of the fake medicine? Or is it the seller of the fake medicine who attacks the doctor who discovered the efficacious medicine? Obviously the seller of the fake medicine has no need to attack the seller of the genuine medicine. It is quite enough for him if the latter refrains from interrogating him or charging him. He is quite happy just to be left alone.

Yet the doctor who distributes the genuine medicine should not and cannot keep silent. For the welfare of the whole city, and in order to save the lives of individual patients, he must take steps against the seller of fake medicine. He must ensure that people are neither deceived by him nor harmed by him. Once you grasp this reasoning you will understand why I cannot do other than oppose those who preach merely the social gospel. They do not attack me first, but they will certainly mount a counter-attack. I recognise that this is inevitable, but I do not shrink from the encounter nor do I seek to evade it. For the sake of the commission that God has entrusted to me, for the protection of the church, for the good of mankind, and for the glory of God – for all these reasons I must oppose the social gospel and warn those who preach it. What else can I do but faithfully transmit the warning that God has uttered through the apostle Paul: 'But even if we, or an angel from heaven, preach any other gospel to you than what we have preached to you, let him be accursed' (Galatians 1: 8).

If you are among those who preach another gospel, will you not turn away from it and escape this terrible curse without delay?

15.
Do not only seek your own interests...

Philippians 2:4

'Let each of you look out not only for his own interests, but also for the interests of others.'

The words in the title of this message are simple, straightforward and commonplace, yet they contain one secret of a successful and overcoming Christian life. A believer needs only to act in accordance with this exhortation and he will be both blessed himself and also be a blessing to others. In addition, he will be widely loved and respected.

It is true of many believers, when they repented and believed, that they gave up many of the sins that they had been in the habit of committing before. No longer do they have anything to do with the shameful and hateful deeds that marked their lives before. But there is one notable shortcoming that remains. It is this. They are concerned only about their own interests; they are not concerned about the interests of others. It is true that they do not get gain for themselves by taking advantage of others, yet they are still mainly concerned with their own interests. Judging by their attitudes, their speech, and their actions, it is evident that they themselves are at the centre. They live only for themselves and all their calculations are with a view to promoting their own interests.

It may be that they are jealous for the truth. It may be that they partake strenuously in the work of God. Externally at least they labour diligently for others. And maybe they gain the respect of those who are superficially acquainted with them. But if they spend any length of time in association with other people then all kinds of difficulties and dissension arise among them. And as a consequence the name of God is dishonoured. In the church there are many people like this. Their need is to give ear to the passage of Scripture quoted above and to learn its valuable lesson deep down in their hearts.

It is not that God forbids us seeking our own interests. So long as we are sojourners in the world we cannot do other than seek our own interests. What God commands is that we should look out not only for our own interests but also for the interests of others. When you are hungry, you need to eat, so if you have food you should go ahead and eat it. But if there are people around who are hungry and have no food you should see to it that they get some too. When you are cold you need clothes to keep you warm. So if you have clothes, then wear them. But if there are people around with insufficient clothes you should see to it that they also are provided with the clothes they need. You yourself need rest; you also need recreation; and this is quite natural. But when you enjoy these things you should ensure that others who need them have the means to enjoy them too. When you yourself encounter adversity you need help to be able to face it. And when those around you encounter adversity you should help them also to face it. When you yourself experience grief you stand in need of comfort; you for your part should be able to comfort other people when grief comes to them.

To seek only your own interests and to ignore the interests of others is pure selfishness. But to seek both your own interests and also the interests of others is to be a good disciple of Christ. Suppose for a moment that God commanded us to seek only the interests of others and not our own interests at all, that would place us in serious difficulty. It would in fact be an impossible situation. But God has not so commanded us. The burden he lays upon us is one that we can bear. Whatever His teaching requires of us it involves nothing beyond our ability. In fact to act in accordance with His requirement can only result in our happiness.

Maybe there are those who question this statement. 'If we seek the interests of others others', they reason, 'we inevitably use up our own strength, our own time, our own resources. this can only involve us in loss. How can you say that it means gains for us and that it results in our happiness?' Those who talk in this way are short-sighted and cannot see what is farther away. Please think! Suppose we are concerned only with our own interests and never show concern for the interests of others, do you imagine that other people will respect us, or love us, or give help to us in time of need? Is it not true that if we do not love others then others will not love us? If we do not seek the interests of others then others naturally will not be concerned about our interests. In time of need we shall forfeit their help, and at all times we shall forfeit their love. What a pitiful state this is for one who is lonely and helpless! Yet it is simply a case of retribution incurred by those who seek only their own interests and not the interests of others.

But let us look at the situation on the reverse side! If we seek not only our own interests but also the interests of others, it will bring its own reward. It is true that among those whom we are able to help some will lack gratitude and will soon forget the help that they have received. But most of them will certainly remember us and the help that they have received, and become our friends. In our own time of need they will help us; in our own time of grief they will comfort us; and in a time of adversity they will stand with us. This should open our eyes to the fact that in seeking the interests of others we are not only bringing happiness to others we are also bringing happiness to ourselves.

Of course, this is not our motive. In seeking the interests of others we do not nourish the hope of being rewarded for it. Yet the God of justice will certainly not leave us without recompense.

The reason that some people are unwilling to take thought for others is certainly that they love only themselves, and that they fear losing out. The unfortunate result is that those who fear loss of this kind will end up by suffering even greater loss. On the other hand, those who are not afraid of suffering loss and who make a point of considering others will gain immeasurably.

How stupid many people are! Not only are they

incapable of loving others but at the same time they show themselves incapable of loving themselves! Of course, the basic reason we give thought for others is that we ourselves are loved by God. Moreover we are taught by the Lord to think of others. But it is a fact – looking at it from the lowest standpoint – that in taking thought for others we are at the same time showing love to ourselves.

When we have made ourselves familiar with the reasoning we ought then – no matter where we are – to give thought to the interests of others. Perhaps for many years we have been accustomed to seeking our own interests only, and as a consequence it will not be easy to get into the habit of considering the interests of other people. Nevertheless we ought not on this account to hesitate and fear. On the one hand we ought to call upon God in His great love to effect a change in us, so that our selfishness gives place to love. And on the other hand we ought to make the effort to correct our selfish habits. Irrespective of whether it is a big matter or a small matter we should be concerned to bring happiness to other people. Whether in the home, or in the church, or in society, no matter what kind of people we associate with, we should in all things pay attention to their needs and to do whatever we can to help them. We should aim to make up for what they lack; we should support them in their weaknesses; we should share their heavy burdens; and we should seek to alleviate their suffering. We should regard helping others as our duty; we should regard receiving help from others as a favour.

Added to all this there is another point that should not be overlooked. It is the need to learn diligence. If we are accustomed to being lazy, and if we are content to continue in that way, we shall never

Is it not like asking a tiger to give up its skin?

develop concern for others. A lazy person cannot be bothered with his own affairs, so how can he be bothered with the affairs of others? A lazy person has to force himself to do what is necessary even for himself. For instance, he finds the preparation of food a bother. But without food he becomes hungry, so he must force himself to prepare his food. But it is only the discomfort of hunger that compels him to act. Consider whether such a man would go out of his way to prepare food for other people – sick people for instance. The same reasoning applies to situations such as providing clothes for those who cannot keep warm in winter or doing the laundry of those unable to do it for themselves. Asking a lazy man to go out of his way in the interests of others – is it not like asking a tiger to give up its skin? The first essential, therefore, is for diligence to replace laziness.

We come back to the fact that it is never easy to get those who habitually seek their own interests to learn concern for others. We cannot learn such concern unless we always keep close to God; unless we always bask in the love of god; and unless we experience the power of God. Whether in the home, in the church, among neighbours or with colleagues, we must always guard against the tendency to gratify our own selfish natures and to ignore the interests of others.

Do not utter words that are harmful to others! Do not engage in projects that are unprofitable for others! Do not encroach on other people's freedom! Do not ride roughshod over other people's privileges! Do not needlessly cause other people to suffer, or give occasion to grieve! Do not be a burden to others! Instead of doing any of these things be always planning to give happiness; to add to others' joy; to lessen others' pain; to satisfy the needs of others; to give comfort to those who are broken-hearted! If there are advantages to be enjoyed, let others go ahead of you. If there are dangers to be faced, let others follow behind you. If you have cause for joy, then share it with others. If others have cause for sorrow, let them share it with you.

But how is it possible to act in this way? You will need very much love and you will need to cultivate the spirit of sacrifice. You must be prepared for self-denial. The result, however, is that you will make other people happy; you will bring glory to God; and you yourself will gain respect. Moreover, when one day you stand before the Lord you will hear Him say to you: 'Well done, good and faithful servant; you have been faithful over a few things, I will make you a ruler over many things. Enter into the joy of your master.'

16.
What is there to fear..?

Isaiah 51:12-15; Psalm 46:1-3, 118:8-14

At the time Isaiah uttered his prophecy the Jews were being invaded by the Babylonians and they were having great difficulty in defending themselves. Their territory had been trampled under foot while their possessions and their people had been taken away. Those whose territory had not yet been violated were filled with terror; they trembled daily lest the threatening Babylonians descend on them suddenly. Yet God had compassion on these Jews for He loved them and it was He who had chosen and saved them. Because of this He spoke through His servant Isaiah, putting a question to them: 'Who are you, that you should be afraid of a man who will die, and of the son

Those who were mortal would change like grass

of a man who will be made like grass; and you forget the Lord your maker, who stretched out the heavens, and laid the foundations of the earth?' In these words He made it known to them that those whom they feared were but mortal and that they would change as easily as grass. Those whom they feared, and whom He compared to grass, had neither power nor authority. If God wills that they die today, none can survive until tomorrow. If God wills that they die in the morning, none can survive until the evening. God asked His people why they feared people like this. He also asked them why they had forgotten that 'Jehovah spreads the heaven and laid the foundation of the earth and created you?' He taught them to bear in mind that only He had ultimate power and authority. By contrasting Himself with those who were mortal and who would change like grass He revealed to them who was great and who was small, who was strong and who was weak. He knew that the reason they feared the Babylonians was simply that they had forgotten Himself; they had forgotten His great power and authority. All that they could think of were the fierce Babylonian armies with their hideous appearance and military might. Therefore He asked them why they feared people like that and why they had forgotten Him. He asked them further, 'Do you fear because the oppressors plot to destroy you?' Finally He asked them 'where is the fury of the oppressor?' He reminded them that although their oppressors were filled with anger, and were indeed bent on exterminating them, without God's permission there was nothing that they could do. After putting these questions to them He continued, 'I am the Lord your God who divided the sea, whose waves roared. The Lord of hosts is his name.' He wanted them to know that His authority was infintely greater than that of the oppressor. Who in all the world had the authority to stir up the ocean? Stirring up the ocean was something quite beyond the power of the Babylonian army and beyond the power of the Babylonian kings. Only God could do this. The God who alone works wonders could keep them so that the oppressor could not harm them. Why should they fear? Finally He uttered a word of great authority and power: 'The Lord of hosts is his name.' Such a word can be compared to streams in the desert and to a great light in the darkness. It is a word that brings great comfort and provides a strong foundation.

This passage with the words of reproof on the one hand and comfort on the other is exactly what is needed by many of God's people at the present time. The news that we now hear, whether in the newspapers or by word of mouth, is both adverse and grievous. It makes everyone fear and tremble. It is as if a great calamity is about to descend upon us. Many believers are as anxious and apprehensive as unbelievers. The oppressor plans destruction and violent anger is about to erupt. In fact in many places it has already erupted. Many have suffered hardship; many have experienced injury; many have known the pungent taste of violence. Destruction is already widespread. 'When the hare dies the fox is sad' (expressing sympathy with one of its kind).

It is only human to be fond of life, to seek happiness and to fear calamity. So how can we reprove people for being alarmed and anxious and sad as they are? No! No! That those who do not believe in God should be like this is not something we can reprove, for they have no one in whom to trust. But those who are Christians are different, and it is not fitting that they should be like this. Through believing in the Lord Jesus Christ we have already become children of God. But God is more than our Father. Psalm 18:2 adds to the picture. 'The Lord is my rock, and my fortress, and my deliverer; my God, my strength, in whom I will trust; my shield, and the horn of my salvation, and my stronghold.' So long as the Lord is with us there is nothing we need fear. Evil men may exhibit violence and cruelty, but they cannot stand against God. Without His permission there is nothing they can do. Even Satan, who governs them, cannot act without the permission of God. He cannot in any way harm those who fear God. God permitted Satan to touch Job's family, but He did not allow Satan to touch Job himself. When eventually God permitted Satan to touch Job's body, He did not permit him to take Job's life (Job 1,2). Even though Satan is prince of the power of the air, without God's permission he cannot bring harm to those who belong to God. Even less can he harm God's messengers. Since this is so, what is there to be afraid of?

So long as we fear men we imply that God is less powerful than men. We under-rate His power. Strictly speaking God should rebuke us and deal with us seriously, but His love is very great, so not only does He refrain from dealing with us in that way, He actually comforts us. 'I, even I, am he who comforts you,' He says. Moreover, gently rebuking us, He enquires: 'Who are you, that you should be afraid of a man who will die, and of the son of a man who will be made as grass?'

Our faith is small; our fears are great. We ought therefore to humble ourselves before God and confess our sin. We ought to entreat Him to have compassion on us and to build up our faith and courage. So long as we keep our eyes on Him, and trust Him with all our heart, we shall not be overcome by fear. Of course, we should always be fearful of falling into sin and of provoking God to anger. But apart from that, what else should we fear.

No! Once we turn our back on fear we can sing with David, 'The Lord is my light and my salvation; whom shall I fear? The Lord is the strength of my life; of whom shall I be afraid?' (Psalm 27:1-3).

17.
What a grave misunderstanding...

Joshua 22: 10–34

The Reubenites, the Gadites, and the half tribe of Manasseh were activated by fear that in days to come the people of the remaining tribes would say that the descendants of these two and a half tribes had no portion in Jehovah. So they set up an altar on the bank of the Jordan according to the patterns of the altars to Jehovah. Without doubt they acted with the best of intentions, and out of consideration for the security and wellbeing of their descendants. There was no element whatever that could rightfully be construed as harmful to other people or offensive to God.

So the outcome was entirely unexpected. As soon

as the members of the other tribes heard what was happening they came to the conclusion that the members of the two and a half tribes were simply erecting an altar for their own personal benefit and rebelling against God. Moved by righteous anger they assembled in Shiloh with the intention of launching an attack against the rebellious people. Fortunately they first sent Phinehas together with ten of the chief men to go and talk to them. As a result they came to understand the true situation and on their return home they explained it to the whole assembly. All the people gave thanks to God, and they gave up completely the idea of going to war with the tribes whom they had previously thought recalcitrant. In other words, the misunderstanding was completely removed and the threatening storm completely stilled. But suppose they had not first despatched the eleven men to make enquiries, and suppose they had precipitately ordered their troops into action, they would certainly have met stiff resistance. For the people of the two and a half tribes were quite unashamed of what they had done; they were not prepared to manifest weakness and they were firmly united in purpose. So had the attack been launched the results do not bear thinking of.

Can we accuse the Reubenites and the Gadites and the half tribe of Manasseh of making a mistake? They were giving thought to the future situation of their descendants and they decided to make provision for them (lit. before the rain). This was a reflection of their deep thinking and of their foresight. And how could they be faulted for that? But when the nine and a half tribes got word of it they concluded that the two and a half tribes were making an altar purely for personal reasons and that they were guilty of rebellion against Jehovah. They had taken warning from the sin of Achan which had implicated the whole body, and they feared that what they regarded as the transgression of the two and a half tribes would implicate the whole body too. They therefore resolved to attack them. On the surface their attitude and their action seemed justifiable.

But was this really so? Consider the viewpoint of the two and a half tribes! Their thinking was quite different from that of the nine and a half tribes. All the tribes had entered Canaan and together they had subdued the tribes of Canaan and occupied the land. Now the nine and a half tribes had divided up the land and were living there peacefully. God's tent of meeting was also set up in Shiloh. It remained for the two and a half tribes to return to the land east of Jordan that Moses had given to them. The river which stretched from north to south was a natural line of demarcation between them and the nine and a half tribes. But on the east side of the River Jordan there was neither a tabernacle nor was there an altar to Jehovah. If in days to come the nine and a half tribes chose to regard the two and a half tribes as having no portion in Jehovah, what could the latter do about it?

The people of the nine and a half tribes who lived peacefully on the west side of the river had given no thought to this problem of the two and a half tribes. Take an illustration. Suppose there are several brothers living together and one of them decides to take his family with him and live elsewhere. As the day for his departure draws near it is natural for him to look ahead to the time of his return. He would ask himself whether at that time there would or would not be a place for him in the home. But what of the brothers in the home who are not moving? Would they not find it difficult to look so far ahead? In exactly the same way people of the nine and a half tribes would find it difficult to think as far ahead as the two and a half tribes. To them the fact that the latter had built an altar could only mean that they had rebelled against Jehovah. What other reason could there be? It was therefore logical for the nine and a half tribes to assemble at Shiloh and to go to war with the two and a half tribes. Thus there was reason on both sides. As a consequence they were all threatened with a storm of the utmost seriousness, and it was all due to a misunderstanding.

Now the fact of a misunderstanding does not necessarily imply the existence of sin. Yet it can result in terrible tragedy. Have we not seen or heard of situations like this? I cannot count the number of times that I myself have seen or heard of them. But in the situation we are consideraing the nine and a half tribes first sent their representative to enquire of the two and a half tribes, and as a result the misunderstanding was removed. The threatening storm died away.

But in the world as we know it today many who are involved in misunderstandings are unwilling to institute enquiries to find out what is the root of their trouble. They hold fast to the opinion that events as they see them are incontravertible facts. They then proceed to act in the light of this. It may mean that they condemn out of hand those whom they have misunderstood and whom they now proceed to attack.

It may be that the people who are the objects of misunderstanding were not originally at fault. But when they are treated unreasonably like this it is not unnatural that they should become upset. They are roused to resist. What follows? Hatred, revenge, quarrelling and fighting all follow in succession. Many troubles and tragedies in the world today are the result of misunderstanding. In many cases the danger could have been removed with clear explanations, but there was no place for this and serious consequences have followed. It is something we must utterly deplore.

When people live together who are different in circumstances, different in background, and different in thinking, it becomes very difficult to avoid misunderstandings. Yet it is not impossible to avoid them. There is, however, only one way to do it. When an issue arises between you and other people which you cannot clear up satisfactorily, you ought to make an effort to find the reason; on no account should you form an opinion prematurely as to what it is all about and then to regard your appraisal as incontestable. For that is how many misunderstandings are brought into existence.

We are well aware that initial judgements must often be modified after we make enquiries. I remember an occasion more than ten years ago, while I was working in Chingdao, when a certain believer invited me to his home for a meal. As we were sitting at the table the host asked me, 'Mr Wong, are those waves in your hair artificial?' I replied, 'Have a guess!' A doctor among the guests then stood up to make a close inspection of my hair. He declared, without hesitation, 'Undoubtedly artificial!' I laughed. 'Have you any grounds,' I asked, 'for saying that they are artificial?' 'I have,' he said. 'Indeed, if the waves are not artificial I will give up being a doctor.' I took him up immediately. 'You have made a slip of the tongue,' I said, 'you'd better quickly withdraw what you said. The waves in my hair are quite natural.' He then added, with considerable disquiet: 'Very strange indeed! Hair with the appearance of yours is exactly like hair waved artificially. How can they possibly be natural waves? I would never have thought it.' Now had my host, on that occasion, not asked the question about my hair the doctor would have expressed his own judgement in the words, 'Mr Wong waves his hair artificially.' How far, do you think, this false report would have spread? Yet this kind of thing is happening all the time. It is not necessary to go as far as discussing things of which we have no direct knowledge, for we well know that the things that we *have* seen and heard often prove to be very different from what at first we thought they were.

Many misunderstandings arise through our failure to consider other people. One of our ancient philosophers once said, 'Being ready at all times to put oneself in the place of others is the highest form of scholarship.' If a healthy man cannot put himself in the place of one who is sick, he can easily misunderstand him. If a man of leisure cannot put himself in the place of one who is extremely busy, he cannot easily understand him. If a guest cannot put himself in the place of a host, it is easy to misunderstand him. If a tenant cannot put himself in the place of a landlord, it is easy to misunderstand him.

Suppose a healthy person is holding a conversation with one who is sick, the sick one, because he lacks strength and because his spirits are low, soon gets weary and begins to doze. The healthy person may get the impression that the sick person is treating him disrespectfully, and misunderstanding arises. Similarly when a man of leisure calls on a busy man, the busy man has no leisure to talk for a long time, and the leisured man gets a wrong impression of the busy man's attitude. Then misunderstanding arises. Again, when a host is entertaining many guests he has

A misunderstanding arises

a good deal to attend to. Should another guest arrive unexpectedly, the host may have to turn away from the others in order to serve the new arrival with tea and cakes. Because of this the other guests may feel offended. And a misunderstanding arises. If only healthy people would put themselves in the place of sick people, if leisured people would put themselves in the place of busy people, and if guests would put themselves in the place of their hosts, then all these misunderstandings could be avoided.

Another cause of misunderstanding is prejudice. For example, some people hold the view that it is impossible for step-mothers to love the children of the former wife of their husband. Because of this the relationship of stepmothers to the children is affected, and other people (and possibly the children themselves) get the impression that the stepmother treats the children harshly. Even when she disciplines them as she should she is regarded as being harsh. All this results from prejudice. Some people think that when their son takes a wife he changes his attitude towards his parents and that he no longer acts in a filial manner. So whenever the son makes a remark that displeases the parents they mistakenly regard him as having changed his attitude towards them as a result of being married. So long as the children are unmarried they may make their parents angry and even bring disgrace on them but the parents invariably overlook it. But as soon as any of the children are married, and take a partner, even though they assiduously carry out their filial duties, their parents still misunderstand them and regard them as being no longer of one spirit with them. This is another example of harm being brought about by prejudice.

As soon as you develop a prejudice against anyone you are liable to misunderstand him. No matter what the latter does he is held to be at fault. A certain householder lost an article of value and he suspected one of his servants of having stolen it. From that time on he regarded that servant as a thief. Whenever the servant appeared to have more money than ususal the master suspected either that he had stolen it or that it was the proceeds of stolen property. The master became more and more obsessed with the idea that the servant was a thief, but because he had no proof he dare not take any action. Then unexpectedly the master came across the article he thought had been stolen and he recalled having put it there himself. He deeply regretted having misunderstood the servant and from that day his whole attitude was changed. Such a situation is far from uncommon. Once we

5

harbour a prejudice against someone, misunderstandings will proliferate. And not until we get rid of the prejudice can we deal with the misunderstanding.

Another major cause of misunderstanding is the failure of people who share the same accommodation to talk with each other sincerely and frankly. It sometimes happens that one person in a group bases his estimate of other people on guesswork and then assumes that his conjectures can on no account be at fault. This may cause many misunderstandings.

It is best, of course, that misunderstandings should not arise, but if they do arise then everything possible should be done to get rid of them before they lead to clashes and strife. The essential factors are honesty, sincerity and frankness. Both sides must speak the truth in love. Had the nine and a half tribes not sent representatives to make enquires of the two and a half tribes (with the resultant clarification of the true function of the altar) it might have been impossible to avoid war with all its misery. But by their action they completely removed the danger of seemingly imminent disaster. Here is an example worth following.

Most people in China set much store on 'face' (i.e. reputation). As a consequence they often act toward each other superficially and deceitfully; while maintaining external courtesies they are unwilling to express what they really feel in their hearts. This is fertile soil for the growth of misunderstandings which may spread beyond control. Let us strive to rid ourselves of all habits that spring from insincerity.

When a person is habitually frank and sincere it is not only easy for him to avoid misunderstanding other people, it is also easier for him to avoid being misunderstood. Those most closely acquainted with him know that they have no cause to doubt what he says. On the other hand the less sincere and frank a person is, the easier it is for misunderstandings to arise, for other people have no idea what he is really thinking. Since a good deal of unhappiness and confusion can be eliminated by sincerity and frankness, why are so many people reluctant to act in this way?

At this point I want to move on and to speak a little about the attitude we ought to adopt when we are misunderstood. Being misunderstood is an experience very hard to endure. Suppose, for instance, you are involved in a situation regarding which you have no evil intent whatsoever yet other people persist in questioning your motives. Perhaps you spend your money liberally on behalf of others, yet you are misunderstood by others who accuse you of fishing for praise and of seeking personal fame. Faced with a situation of this nature you are sad and grieved, and it is easy to get angry and to blame people for not appreciating your sincerity. You may even begin to hate those who misunderstand you and to contemplate retaliation. When the situation reaches this point, if you do not 'rein in your horse as you approach the precipice' you will set in motion a sequence of harmful events that you never dreamed possible.

When you are misunderstood and misfortunes follow, it is well for you to remember that it is not a case of others groundlessly mistreating you. It is basically that they misunderstand you and in their minds, they are fully convinced that their understanding of the situation is accurate. They thus regard you as being entirely in the wrong, and on this basis they will oppose you and even denounce you. Should you on your part misunderstand them by regarding them as nurturing evil, your natural reaction is to oppose them and to attack them in the same way that they have attacked you.

I know a certain sister in the Lord who once became the target of another person's hate and hate-inspired insults. She was certainly not at fault in the matter and it was plainly a case of the other person misunderstanding her. As I observed the way things were developing I was increasingly disturbed. But this is what the sister said to me: 'You shouldn't be angry about this. The fact that she hates me and insults me as she does is not a case of acting groundlessly. It is true that she misunderstands me, but her treatment of me is based on the fact that she regards me as having acted wrongly. Thus her treatment of me is not arbitrary. Had she not first misunderstood me she would not have acted towards me as she did.'

What this sister said to me was certainly true. If we, when we are misunderstood, can adopt the same attitude as this sister, not only shall we save ourselves considerable suffering, we shall also remove the risk of much misfortune.

Who in the history of the world has been more misunderstood than God? God's love is far greater than any human love, and He treats people infinitely better than any human being. Yet He rarely gets expressions of gratitude, and He is constantly misunderstood. He is misunderstood, on the one hand, by those who neither believe Him nor worship Him; He is misunderstood, on the other hand, by His own children. The grace with which He has treated mankind is higher than the heavens and broader than the earth, yet only a few people in the world pause to thank Him. There are few who sing His praises. At the same time those who hate and slander Him are as numerous as the sands on the banks of the Ganges.

151

Christian believers also err in this way. When their circumstances are adverse they begin to grumble against God and inwardly accuse Him of lack of mercy and lack of justice. Yet God never shows anger against people like this. He treats them unfailingly with love and patience and generosity. I hope that they will come to realise this.

The children of God ought to act in the same way as God towards those who misunderstand them,. The fact that God has taught us to be like Him makes this reasoning even stronger.

In summary, then, I say that we ought to be very careful that we do not misunderstand other people. And when we ourselves are misunderstood we ought to act magnanimously and to forgive those who misunderstand us. At the same time we must use every opportunity to remove all misunderstanding. If we do this we shall experience more of God's grace and more of man's love. And at the same time we shall be acknowledged by the Lord Jesus Christ as disciples pleasing to Him.

18.
Why did Jesus first appear to a disciple like this...

Matthew 26: 69–75
Luke 24: 33,34
1 Corinthians 15: 3–5

Three times did Peter deny his Lord. Such an action was not only a sign of ingratitude, it was also extremely shameful and cowardly. To deny one's Lord once may be regarded as due to a moment's weakness, but what can be said to excuse repeated acts of this kind? He not only denied that he was a disciple of Jesus, he even declared, 'I do not know the man'. Added to all that, he accompanied his statement with oaths and curses. Humanly speaking, to offend the Lord and to wound the Lord in the way he did was a sin which could on no account be treated

Before the cock crows thou shalt deny me thrice

leniently. It was therefore very strange that of the apostles to whom the Lord revealed himself when he rose from the dead, it was Peter to whom He revealed Himself first.

Why should this be? In order to answer this question we must first consider the feelings that swept through Peter's heart after his failure. What does Scripture tell us? 'Peter remembered the word of Jesus, which said unto him, Before the cock crow, thou shalt deny me thrice. And he went out, and wept bitterly.'

At the time of Peter's grief his Lord was still in the courtyard of the High Priest. Just imagine what he must have felt like when his Lord was crucified! From the time of his denial he had had no time to confess his failure to the Lord. For the Lord was led from the courtyard of the High Priest to that of Pontius Pilate; He was then taken to Golgotha where He was crucified.

Peter really loved his Lord. Yet he saw Him subjected to all kinds of suffering and shame, and He was then tragically put to death. Every event on that day was enough to break Peter's heart, but what brought him the greatest sorrow at that time was the fact that although he had denied his Lord with oaths and curses, he had had no opportunity, from beginning to end, to confess his sin to the Lord and to seek His forgiveness. The state of Peter's heart during the three days that Jesus spent in the tomb may well be imagined. Among the disciples there was probably not one who grieved more, or who was more broken-hearted, or more full of contrition than Peter. So when the Lord showed Himself first to Peter, after He had risen from the dead, it was because He knew that Peter was in particular need of comfort and support. 'A bruised reed he will not break, smoking flax he will not quench' (Isaiah 42: 3). Peter at that time was exactly like the bruised reed and the smoking flax.

In appearing first to Peter the Lord was simply letting Peter know that his grief and repentance were known to Him and that his sin was already forgiven. It was also to let Peter know that although he had been overcome by fear and had lacked courage to confess his Lord, from beginning to end the Lord's love had not in any way changed.

By this time Peter no longer needed to be

reproved. The rebuke that he had given himself was already sufficiently severe. What he now needed was to be soothed and comforted; he needed compassion and forgiveness. Thus the Lord appeared to him first in order to comfort him in his grief and to revive his spirit. This demonstration of the Lord's overwhelming love inspired him as nothing else could have done. It made him willing to give up all for his Lord, to endure being wronged, to go forth in service for the Lord, and if need be to lay down his life.

In the Church today there are many saints like Peter. In a moment of weakness they stumble and fall; they are guilty of giving offence to their Lord. But afterwards they repent of their failure and suffer pain and grief on account of it. They get to hate themselves and to rebuke themselves. Such a situation can easily result in their being discouraged to the point of despair. At such a time their greatest need is to become aware of the Lord's forgiveness and pardon; to become conscious of the Lord's compassion and love; and to have their wounds treated with precious ointment.

Unfortunately there are many zealous Christians, and even Christian preachers, who when confronted by believers like Peter can only rebuke them for their sin. Sometimes they go even further and look down upon them, condemn, and leave them to their own devices. Yet the believers concerned, like Peter, have long before repented of their sin and severely rebuked themselves. In their grief they fear that the Lord will not forgive them and that consequently He will abandon them. If, in addition to that, they are compelled to listen to the reproaches of other believers and even to incur their dislike, they will be even more discouraged and tempted to despair. Satan will then have another opportunity to accuse them, attacking them with the insinuation that they have disqualified themselves from being forgiven and that never again can they be pleasing to the Lord. When they come under multiple attack like this their situation is beyond imagination. To sum up, this is truly a sad situation, greatly to be deplored. By a quirk of reasoning those most disparaging of those who have stumbled are often found among the more zealous believers, who come to dislike not only the sin but the sinner also. The cold-hearted on the other hand show no particular antipathy to the sin or to the sinners involved.

What it means is that some of the more zealous believers are not sufficiently forbearing and that they do not give the erring ones sufficient opportunity to repent. In their view, it is only those who had not previously been Christians who are in a position, on repenting and confessing their sin before the Lord, to expect forgiveness. As for those who were already believers, even though they repent, there is no such hope. In fact when you observe the severe attitude that some of them adopt towards the erring you gain the impression that they are more to be feared than the Lord Himself.

I am not saying that we should never reprove believers who fall into sin. If those who fall into sin show no sign of repenting and confessing their sin, they are naturally in need of rebuke and warning. But I am speaking now of those who, although they have erred, do not wait to be reproved by others but who are already deeply repentant. They confess their sin; they rebuke themselves and hate themselves for it. In that respect they are like Peter who went out and wept bitterly. What they now need is not rebuke and warning; they need sympathy and comfort. What they need is to be reminded of Psalm 51: 17: 'The sacrifices of God are a broken spirit; a broken and contrite heart – These you will not despise.' What they need is to be reminded of Isaiah 1: 18: 'Come now, and let us reason together, says the Lord: though your sins are like scarlet, they shall be white as snow; though they be red like crimson, they shall be as wool.' What they need is to be reminded that 'If we confess our sins, he is faithful and just to forgive us our sins, and to cleanse us from all unrighteousness' (1 John 1: 9), and that 'If anyone sins, we have an advocate with the Father, Jesus Christ the righteous' (1 John 2: 1).

Now what about you who are reading this message? Have you cause to be sad at heart? Have you reason to rebuke yourself and hate yourself? If so, I urge you to look away to the Lord and to ponder His inexhaustible love. The Lord will no more reprove you than He reproved Peter. On the contrary He will pardon you as He pardoned Peter. The Lord who showed His concern for Peter, in appearing to him before He appeared to others, will likewise show His concern for you. Not only will He refrain from breaking the bruised reed, He will support it and enable it to stand up again. Not only will He refrain from quenching the smoking flax, He will, on the contrary, pour on oil. No one in the world can forgive sin as He does. No one in the world can comfort the broken-hearted as He does. No one in the world can wipe away the tears as He does. No one in the world can understand man's weaknesses as He does. No one hates sin as He does. No one loves all men as He does. No one can compare with Him for holiness and justice; no one can compare with Him for meekness and compassion. Jesus will receive men though no one else will receive them. Jesus will act large-heartedly though no one else will do so.

True, when it comes to dealing with people who are

obstinate, Jesus will be very severe. But when it comes to those who humble themselves and confess their sin – those who mourn for their sin and repent of it – Jesus will treat them with boundless compassion.

No matter who turns against you, you need not be discouraged. No matter who condemns you, you need not be afraid. So long as the Lord Jesus does not condemn you and reject you, you may be at peace. You may lift up your head. Do not turn your eyes to the frowning features of men; fix your gaze on the smiling face of the Lord. Do not open your ears to the threatening words of men; listen, rather, to the compassionate voice of the Lord. Peter's master is also *our* master. Arise! Let us be going!

19.
A wise leader...

2 Samuel 12: 7–15
1 Kings 1: 32–35

The qualities of wisdom and greatness, in David, are easily discernible in the above two passages of Scripture. After David had plotted to cause harm to Uriah and to take his wife, Bath-sheba, for himself, he was visited by the prophet Nathan. The prophet was in no way deterred by feelings of sentiment and speaking out in the name of the Lord he reproved David for his sin. Any other king but David, confronted by a prophet in this way, might conceivably have restrained himself from flying into a rage and becoming violent, but he would hardly have avoided nourishing resentment. He would have awaited an opportunity to launch an attack on the prophet; at least he would have avoided the prophet lest he again be rebuked and put to shame. But David was different. Not only did he forbear from acting in any of these ways, but when the time came for his son Solomon to succeed him, David sent Nathan the prophet with Zadok the priest to anoint him as king over Israel. So even on an important occasion like this it was not a relative but a prophet – one who would administer justice without partiality – to whom he entrusted this meaningful task. The significance lies in the fact that it was this very prophet who had rebuked David severely on account of his sin and who had announced the curses imposed by God. Apart from David how many would have been both able and willing to act in this way? Merely a handful. Yet people who do act like this are undoubtedly pleasing to God and qualified to be His instruments.

To accept the rebuke of other people is not an easy thing to do. To appreciate and to approach those who have rebuked you is even harder. Only the humblest people are able to act in this way and only the wisest of people are willing to act in this way. But those who do so are set to make spiritual progress and to grow more holy. They will not easily be curbed by those who are petty-minded. They will not easily become the instruments of Satan. They will avoid many dangers. They will be greatly blessed by God. It will be evident that they are both great and wise. But those who are willing to act in this way, alas!, are as rare as stars in the morning.

Most people like to be esteemed and respected. so when you come across people who esteem and respect you, you act towards them in a friendly way and you are happy to associate with them. Appearances are, however, deceptive. What appears on the surface to be esteem and respect may actually emanate from petty-mindedness and selfishness. By flattering and eulogising you, a person may really be aiming to secure some benefit. You are naturally pleased to be flattered and eulogised, but the end result may involve harm to all concerned.

Far different from flatterers are people who are prepared to exhort you and if necessary to reprove you in person. They seek no personal benefit and they are both upright and courageous. If they see you making mistakes they will speak to you frankly in the hope that you will change your ways. If you for your part are amenable to admonition, your faults will diminish and your character will develop. The fact that David pleased God was not of course due to the attitude we are now reviewing by itself. But undoubtedly the fact that he continued to have contact with Nathan in spite of being rebuked by him, was one of the more important reasons.

This is certainly a remarkable quality. It is also the mark of a special gift from God. Another point to be noticed is that we are thinking about a man who carried heavy responsibilities and whose ministry had widespread importance. The manner of his administration would affect the security or otherwise of many people while his words and deeds would have a bearing on people's welfare, determining their happiness or misery. Even a minor transgression on David's part would have wide implications.

Nathan was a loyal and courageous prophet. David was a devout and humble king. Through these two men the whole community of Israel was greatly blessed.

Alas! Irrespective of whether you speak in terms of the nation or of society or of the church, there are very few leaders today like David. It is true even in the Church that many leaders show tendencies to favour those who flatter them or praise them. Should any of these leaders exhibit shortcomings, or make mistakes, they tend to favour those who cover them up – just as the cicada ceases to utter sounds in cold weather. But so long as leaders welcome and even make use of people like this how can the affairs they manage be other than bungled – whether in the nation or in society or in the Church?

The fact is that whether in society, nation, or Church there are leaders whose aim is to achieve fame and to accumulate wealth. For leaders like this the concepts of righteousness and truth do not exist. Such people are totally incapable of giving heed even to reproofs made in sincerity. They have to be left to the judgement of God.

I can recall situations that are even more tragic. The leaders originally loved truth and righteousness and they desired to do something both for God and for man. But then something happened. They discontinued their association with people who were honest and upright and began to associate with petty-minded people who were given to both slander and flattery. As a result these leaders totally undermined the work that deep down in their hearts they really wanted to carry out. And they remained in complete ignorance of the many people whom they had injured. How painful it is just to recall such a happening!

Some of the Western brothers and sisters who preach the Gospel in our country have made mistakes like this, and not a few cases of this are known to me personally. The more zealous these Western workers are, and the more they love the Lord, the easier it seems for them to fall into this kind of error. One reason for this is that since they themselves are sincere and devout they regard others as sincere and devout like themselves. The thought never occurs to them that while the speech of some people is utterly convincing, in their hearts they are utterly ruled by evil. In the hearts of these Western workers there is no thought of deceit, they therefore regard other people as also being without deceit. These workers have no intention whatever of taking advantage of people, and they therefore regard others as being free from this intention also. What it all amounts to is that their goodness of heart has paved the way for them to be cheated by people who are petty-minded,

Even these excellent Western workers, however, are not entirely free from blame in allowing themselves to be hoodwinked by evil men. Their mistake likes in allowing themselves to develop an undue liking for those who follow thier own bent of mind and in disliking those people – basically upright – who express different opinions from them and who raise questions as to their actions.

Yet it is virtually impossible for everybody in a group of fellow-workers to hold identical opinions to all the others. Situations are bound to arise when differences of opinion come to the surface. In such a situation those who are under authority should be allowed absolute freedom to express their views in the presence of those in authority, and to be able to do so without the slightest fear of incurring disfavour. Those in positions of leadership should be particularly appreciative and respectful of people who differ from them.

Alas! Many leaders are not like this. When they are confronted by fellow-workers who are frank and forthright – albeit utterly sincere – they tend to show displeasure. At the same time they are invariably favourably disposed towards those who follow them without raising questions. In such an atmosphere the point is inevitably reached when someone becomes aware of what he regards as a faulty move on the part of a leader and cannot restrain himself from remonstrating with him. This is often more than leaders can tolerate, for they look upon this as representing a hostile attitude and as failure to submit to authority. As soon as such a suspicion arises the leaders deliberately avoid such people. They may even go so far as to expel them. The end result is that people who are upright and faithful withdraw while the crafty remain.

Many devout Western missionaries come to China prepared to suffer hardship. They labour for many years and in the course of their work they spend a great deal of money. Yet sometimes the outcome of all their labour is just a thick register containing many names, a large chapel where birds can nest in the entrance, and the well-dressed families of several Chinese preachers. In addition there are young people who, having been supported in their studies by Westerners will go out after graduation and declaim against those missionaries.* On the one hand I feel very deeply for those Western missionaries but on the other hand I cannot do other than recognise that they often brought such trouble on themselves. Had they only adopted the same attitude towards questioning Chinese believers as David did towards Nathan they could have escaped being overtaken by such an unhappy state of affairs.

And why stop at Western leaders? Are not many of the Chinese leaders in the churches just the same? So long as they had neither position nor authority maybe they were still willing to accept admonition and to heed warning from other people. But once they are placed in a position of authority, especially after an experience of success, it becomes easy for their hearts to be lifted up with pride. They become intolerant of suggestions put forward by others and reject out of hand even faithful words of remonstrance. While they are still open to accept flattery and commendation, they dislike and disdain honest speech and faithful expostulation. It is then that the faithful and upright ones are obliged to move away. In a situation like this, if the leaders do not awake to a sense of their own shortcomings and repent – 'drawing in the reins on approaching the precipice' – they will inevitably be plunged into failure. The church will suffer loss and the Lord's name will be dishonoured. These are circumstances that I myself have seen not infrequently in various churches.

Some leaders put the blame for such developments on the unwillingness of certain people to help them. And I have to admit – Alas! – that it is impossible to avoid being criticised by people who are self-seeking and cunning. But I still maintain that the gravest error normally lies with the leaders themselves. If you put a pot of fragrant flowers in your courtyard you will probably have many beautiful butterflies hovering around it. But if you put a bowl of putrid meat there it will attract a swarm of flies enough to make one vomit. To exonerate leaders from all blame is like blaming butterflies for not coming into the courtyard instead of blaming oneself for not putting out fresh flowers; and like blaming the flies for swarming in the home instead of blaming oneself for putting out putrid meat. So long as a leader keeps an open mind and is prepared to listen to sincere remonstrance, then he will be surrounded by people of integrity. But if a leader gives ear to flattery and if at the same time he refuses to heed good counsel, preferring to gloss

Flagrant flowers will attract beautiful butterflies

over his mistakes, he will be surrounded by people who are deceitful and crafty.

History teaches us that there have been kings who were themselves originally high-minded, but because they put their trust in people who were unworthy, and because they were pleased to listen to flattery, they bungled the affairs of state beyond recovery and they themselves came to tragic ends. A similar situation is found in certain churches today. Deceitful and ungodly men, followers of Judas, have been set up by the leaders as pillars in the church, and it thus becomes a nest for the devil. What anguish we suffer when we observe a situation like this!

I would very much like to preach in more detail of David's confidence in Nathan, so that we all might become more familiar with this most important qualification for leadership. But alas! I do not have the opportunity. And even if I did have the opportunity, how many would listen?

*At times, when anti-foreign feeling ran high, the·graduates of Mission schools often felt that they had to do something to stress their patriotism to offset any stigma resulting from their being educated at foreigners' expense – Translator.

20.
Smooth Stones...

1 Samuel 17: 38–40, 48–51

All readers of the Old Testament are familiar with the story of David and Goliath. Goliath was the champion of the Philistines and he was feared by the whole army of Israel. Yet David killed him and so delivered the people of Israel from the Philistines. He did it with one small stone. Strange! Truly strange! The potentiality of one small stone was so vast that it could achieve deliverance for all the people of Israel. Obviously an important factor in this achievement was the skill of David in slinging stones. But most important of all was the fact that this was a marvellous act of God. For in effecting this deliverance God needed only one small stone to kill the champion – the fierce champion from whom everybody fled in fear. Similarly, when God effects deliverance today He can use even the weakest of believers to achieve that which, without Him, is impossible even for an army.

The people around David were under the impression that only the use of the sword and spear and javelin could defeat a powerful enemy. But God made use of what man overlooked – a stone. Nowadays there is a commom impression that it is only people with learning and ability and position and wealth who can achieve anything great. But God uses believers who are foolish and weak and poor and lowly to do wonderful things for Him. 'God hath chosen the foolish things of the world to confound the things which are mighty; and base things of the world, and things which are despised, hath God chosen, yea, and things which are not, to bring to nought things that are; that no flesh should glory in his presence' (1 Corinthians 1: 27–29). God could do wonderful things like this in days of old; He can do wonderful things today. He alone is worthy to be praised.

At the same time we are confronted here with a certain factor which we must not lightly dismiss. It is that when God used David to kill Goliath, the stones that David used were not ordinary stones; they were 'smooth stones' specially selected from the brook. Now the stones which lay in the brook were far too numerous to be counted; yet only a few of them were suitable for David's sling. Before David could go to the field of battle he had to make his way first to the brook and from the thousands of stones which lay there to select five smooth stones for his sling. He had to aim accurately and to hit the enemy's forehead. The stones had to be smooth. We must remember, however, that the process of making these stones smooth enough for use could not be compressed into

Smooth stones from the brook

a day. On the contrary it would require years and years of preparation.

The stones that we find in brooks or on the sea shore were originally thrown out as a result of huge explosions amongst the rocks. But all these stones at that time had sharp edges and corners. Not one of them was smooth. But as the flowing water swept over them they were constantly rubbing each other. In this way the corners were gradually rubbed off. As the process continued for thousands of years the stones in time became perfectly smooth. Now we often pick up stones like this both from streams and from the sea shore. But do we ever stop to think of the long process of friction which has made them so smooth? The more these stones were thrown together the more their corners were worn off and the smoother they became. At the same time they became more beautiful and more useful. Since stones are inanimate objects they have no feeling, and naturally we never associate the smoothing process with pain. But if stones had feeling when they were in collision with each other for such a long time I honestly do not know to what degree their suffering would extend.

The people whom God chooses and uses are in a similar situation. They have been saved, and the sins of the past have been forgiven, but many corners remain in their make-up. They are things like laxity, pride, selfishness, covetousness, envy and hatred. Unless these corners are submitted to a long process of rubbing and buffeting they will not easily be removed.

The question arises, what does God make use of to carry out this process of rubbing? He uses the people around us. That which ceaselessly rubs and polishes a stone is not soil, sand, bricks, or pieces of wood; even less is it grass, leaves, cotton wadding, or sheep's wool. None of these things is hard like the stone. And none of them will ever rub off the corners. The stones are made smooth because they are constantly rubbed by other stones – vast numbers of them. Only hard things can wear out hard things. When the mountain torrents catch up the small stones and sweep them together they gradually lose their corners.

In the same way, for the corners in our personalities to be rubbed off we need to be thrown together with other people. I buffet you; you buffet me. By nature we like to live with people who are meek, peaceable, humble, patient, compassionate and benevolent. But God seems to go out of His way, as it were, to put us in the midst of people who are evil, violent, proud, irritable, self-centred and cruel. We murmur against God for not treating us more kindly; we lament that our lot is unpleasant; and we long to get release from our situation. We fail to perceive that God has purposely placed us in the midst of people like this so that the corners in our personalities, of which He is well aware, may in course of time be rubbed completely off. Without treatment like this the corners will remain. If you put a small stone with edges and corners into a ball of cotton wadding, even if it remains there for hundreds of years, the corners will not be worn down in the slightest. In the same way, if we live always among virtuous people our corners will remain with us – even perhaps until the Lord returns.

We often wonder why God persists in keeping us in unpleasant surroundings, in making us mix with unattractive people. For instance a man by nature wishes to take a wife who is virtuous and wise and submissive, yet contrary to his wishes the wife he marries is fierce and excitable. A woman by nature wishes to be married to a man who is gentle and considerate, but contrary to her desire she finds herself married to one who is churlish and rude. An elderly woman looks for a daughter-in-law who is filial and dutiful; but contrary to her hopes her son takes a wife who has no respect for her superiors. A young wife hopes to have a kindly mother-in-law, but contrary to her hopes she finds her husband's mother to be unreasonable and truculent. Masters desire servants who are loyal and obedient, but those they employ prove to be deceitful, cunning, and depraved. Servants wish to work for kind and considerate masters, but invariably they are cruel and repressive. Landlords fail to find good tenants; tenants fail to find good landlords. Superior government officials cannot find good subordinates; subordinate officials look in vain for good superiors.

So the general situation is most unsatisfactory. Reality rarely matches the ideal. God appears to be hostile to us and purposely loading us with trouble. But as soon as we understand the significance of the smooth stones our many suspicions completely vanish. Some of the people in our families are hard to get along with, and some of the people who share our courtyards are hard to live with, but God has expressly placed us among them so that they may help to rub off our edges and corners. In this situation all that we can do is to maintain thankful and obedient hearts and to endure the inevitable buffeting so that in the end we may become like smooth stones. We shall then be of great potential usefulness to the Lord.

Even though people treat us roughly, once we have understood the significance of the stones we shall cease to murmur against God. No more shall we opt prematurely out of our situation or seek to avoid the people who do not appeal to us. We accept God's perfect will and endure what He sends so that He can make us into smooth stones all the sooner. The pain which this prolonged buffeting brings to us may indeed be intense, but the advantages we gain by paying this price are such as can never be bought by silver or gold.

There are so many stones in the brook that you cannot count them. Yet in every ten you cannot find more than one or two that are useable. There was no room in David's pouch for the stones which had not been polished smooth. The process of attrition was essential. In the same way those believers who have not yet experienced trials and afflictions, and who have not yet been disciplined by God, are still not ready for His use.

We have seen, then, that David had to select five smooth stones from the brook before he went out to do battle. The question now before me is whether God, from this great gathering of believers, can choose five who are polished and smooth and prepared like the five stones of David. What I am even more anxious to know is whether I myself am qualified to be a 'smooth stone' in the hand of God.